AF576510

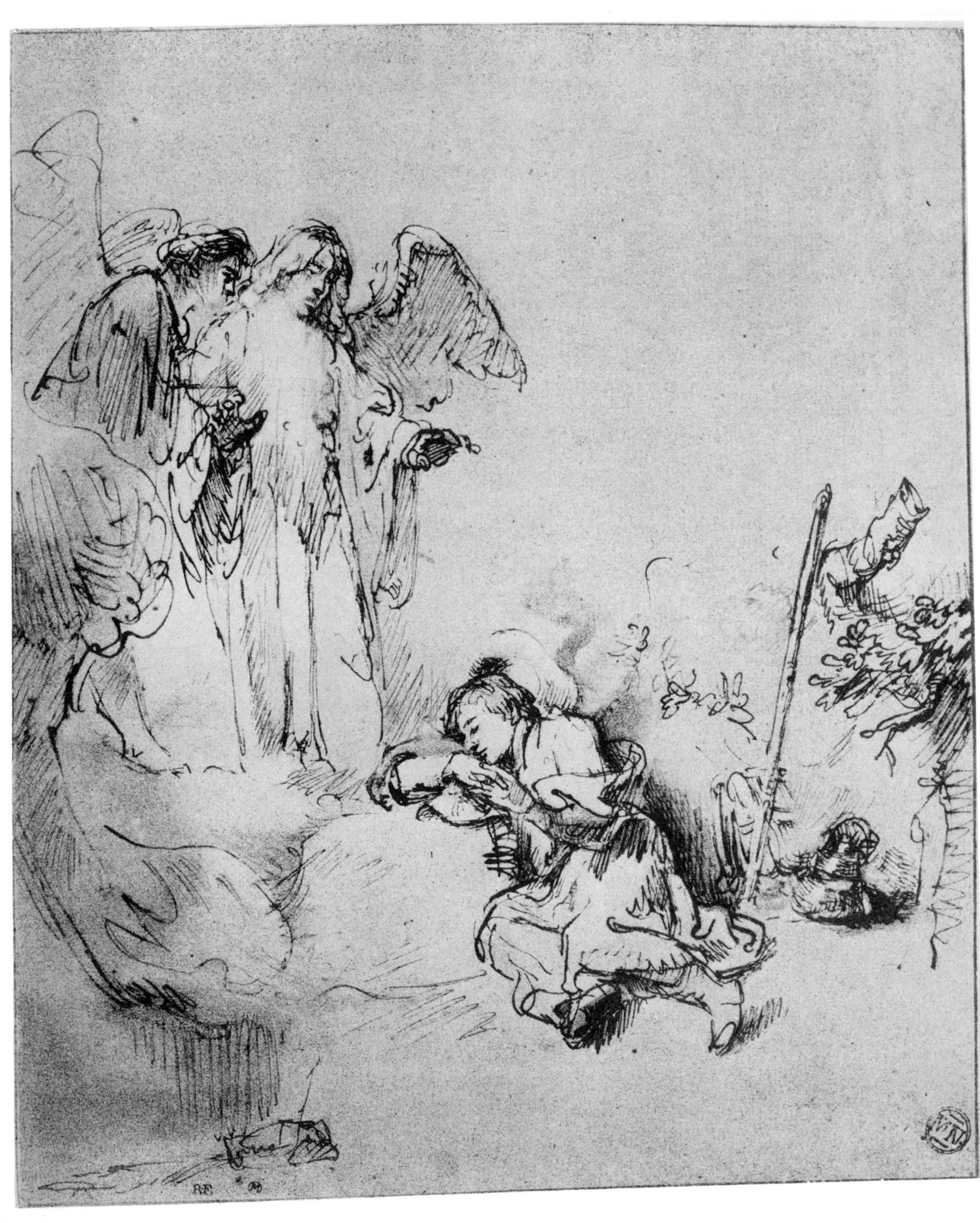

Jacob's Dream. Ca. 1640. Pen and wash in bistre, corrections in white body color. 205 x 208 mm. Louvre, Paris.

REMBRANDT
BIBLE DRAWINGS

60 Works by
Rembrandt van Rijn

Dover Publications, Inc., New York

Publisher's Note

For many art lovers, Rembrandt van Rijn (1606–1669) remains the supreme draftsman, as much for his immense technical skill as for his profound insight into human behavior and interrelationships. Nowhere are these gifts more in evidence than in his Biblical studies, which comprise the largest single group among his extant drawings. The Bible nourished Rembrandt's imagination throughout his artistic development, and the works included in the present volume range from his breathtakingly virtuosic sketches of the early 1630s, vibrant with somewhat melodramatic joy and sorrow, to the monumentally calm and firm compositions of his final years. Not many Rembrandt drawings can be directly identified as preliminary sketches for engravings or paintings; even though not highly finished, they were largely created for their own sake. The artist would return repeatedly to the same Biblical passages, setting himself new challenges in the interpretation of the great book.

In this volume, the scenes, none of which is represented more than once, occur in their sequence within the Bible; for scenes derived from the Gospels, the sequence follows the scheme: The Life of St. John the Baptist, The Life of Christ, The Teaching of Christ, Parables, Miracles, The Passion of Christ. No drawing is included that is not considered perfectly genuine by the major Rembrandt scholars Otto Benesch and Seymour Slive. The original dimensions of the drawings are given in millimeters, height before width.

Published in Canada by General Publishing Company, Ltd., 30 Lesmill Road, Don Mills, Toronto, Ontario.
Published in the United Kingdom by Constable and Company, Ltd., 10 Orange Street, London WC2H 7EG.

Rembrandt Bible Drawings, first published by Dover Publications, Inc., in 1979, is a new selection of drawings reproduced from a variety of sources. The identifications of the subjects, and the captions, are based on those in the two-volume work *Drawings by Rembrandt*, by Seymour Slive, published by Dover Publications, Inc., in 1965; and in *The Drawings of Rembrandt; A Critical and Chronological Catalogue*, by Otto Benesch, 6 vols., London, 1954–57. The Publisher's Note has been prepared specially for the present edition.

International Standard Book Number: 0-486-23878-4
Library of Congress Catalog Card Number: 79-52975

Manufactured in the United States of America
Dover Publications, Inc.
180 Varick Street
New York, N.Y. 10014

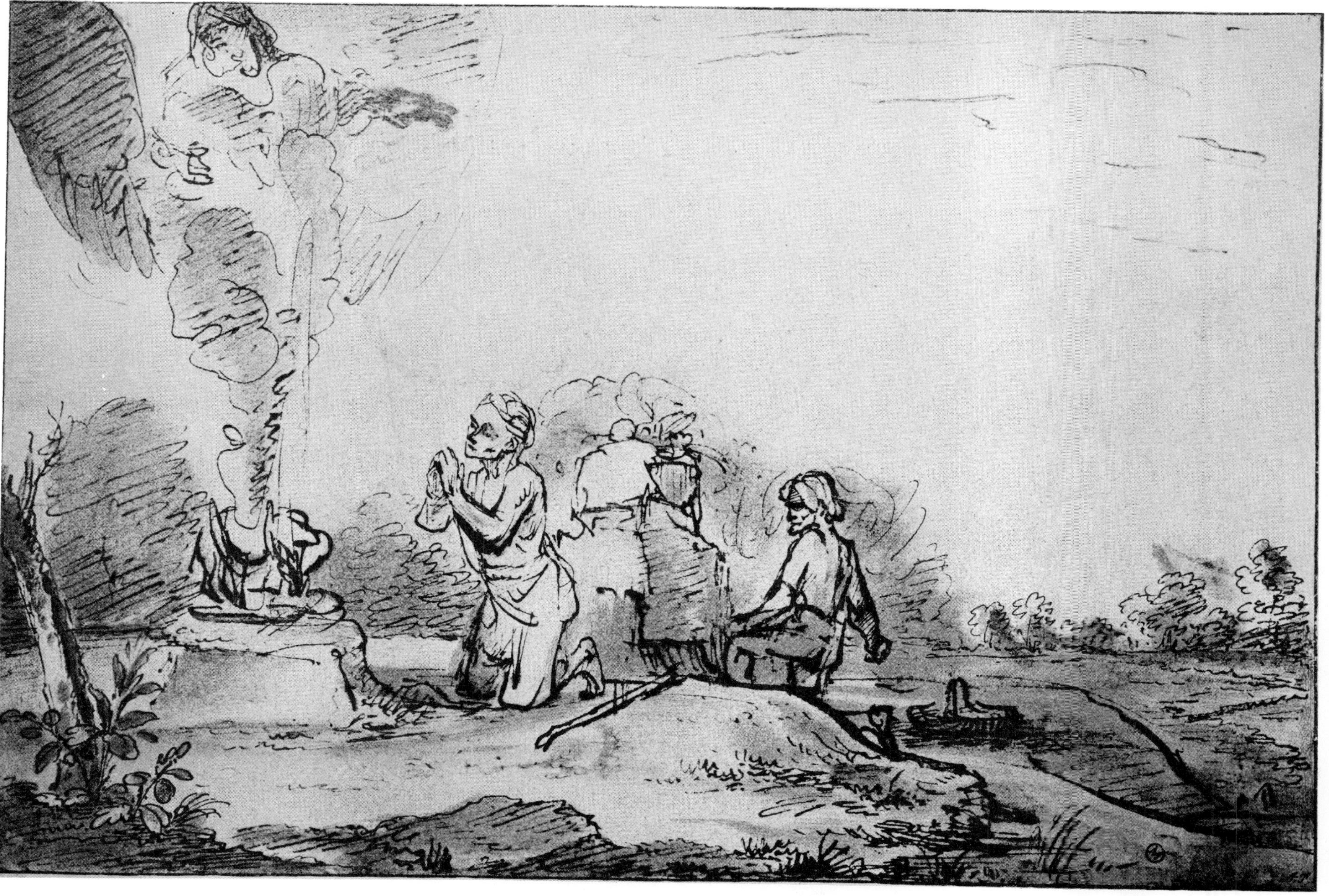

1. The Offerings of Cain and Abel. Ca. 1650. Pen and wash in bistre, white body color. 197 x 295 mm. Kupferstichkabinett, Berlin. The background landscape, the tree trunk and some of the clouds are by another hand.

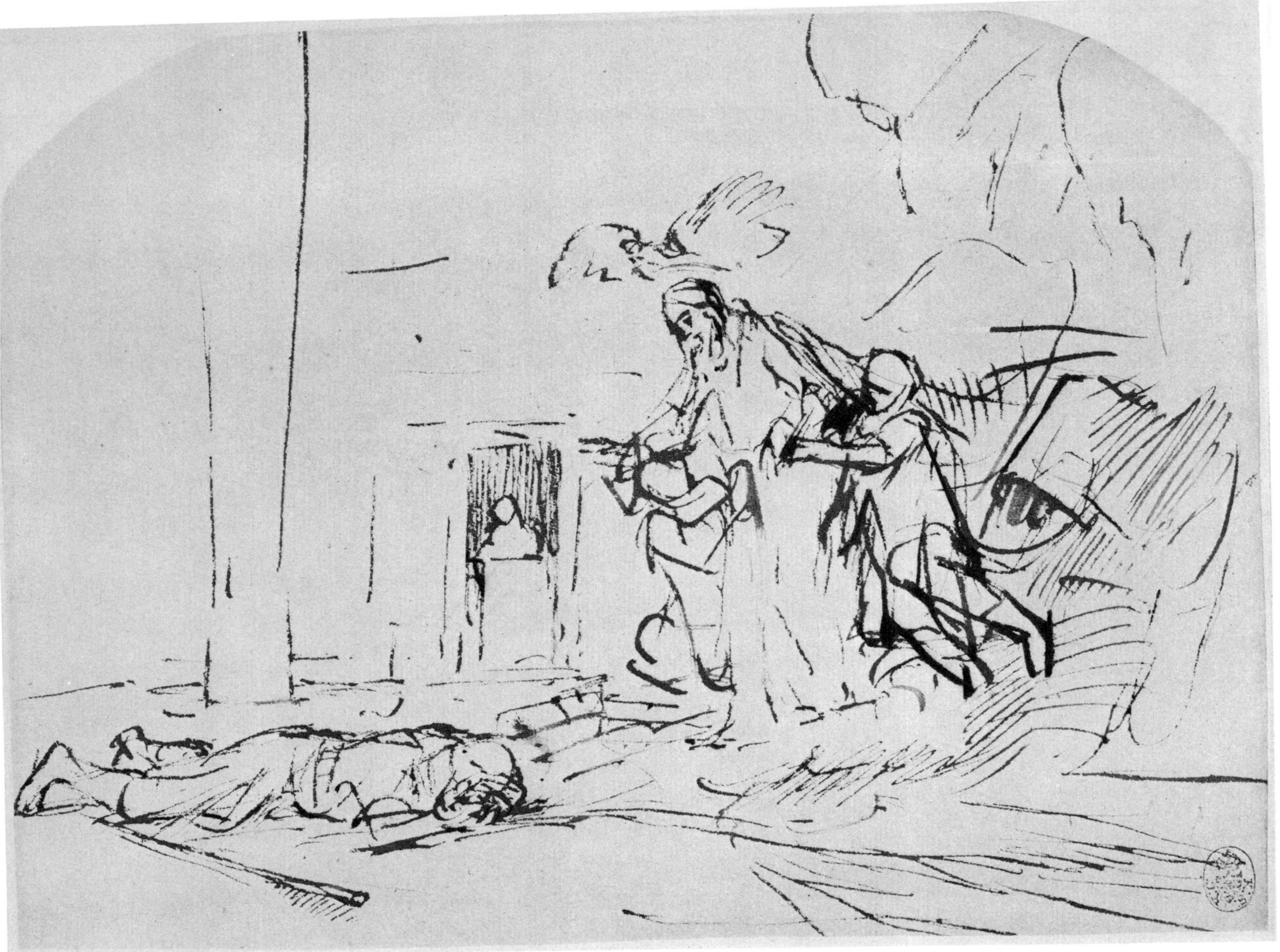

2. God Announces His Covenant to Abraham. Ca. 1657. Pen and bistre. 197 x 266 mm. Kupferstichkabinett, Dresden.

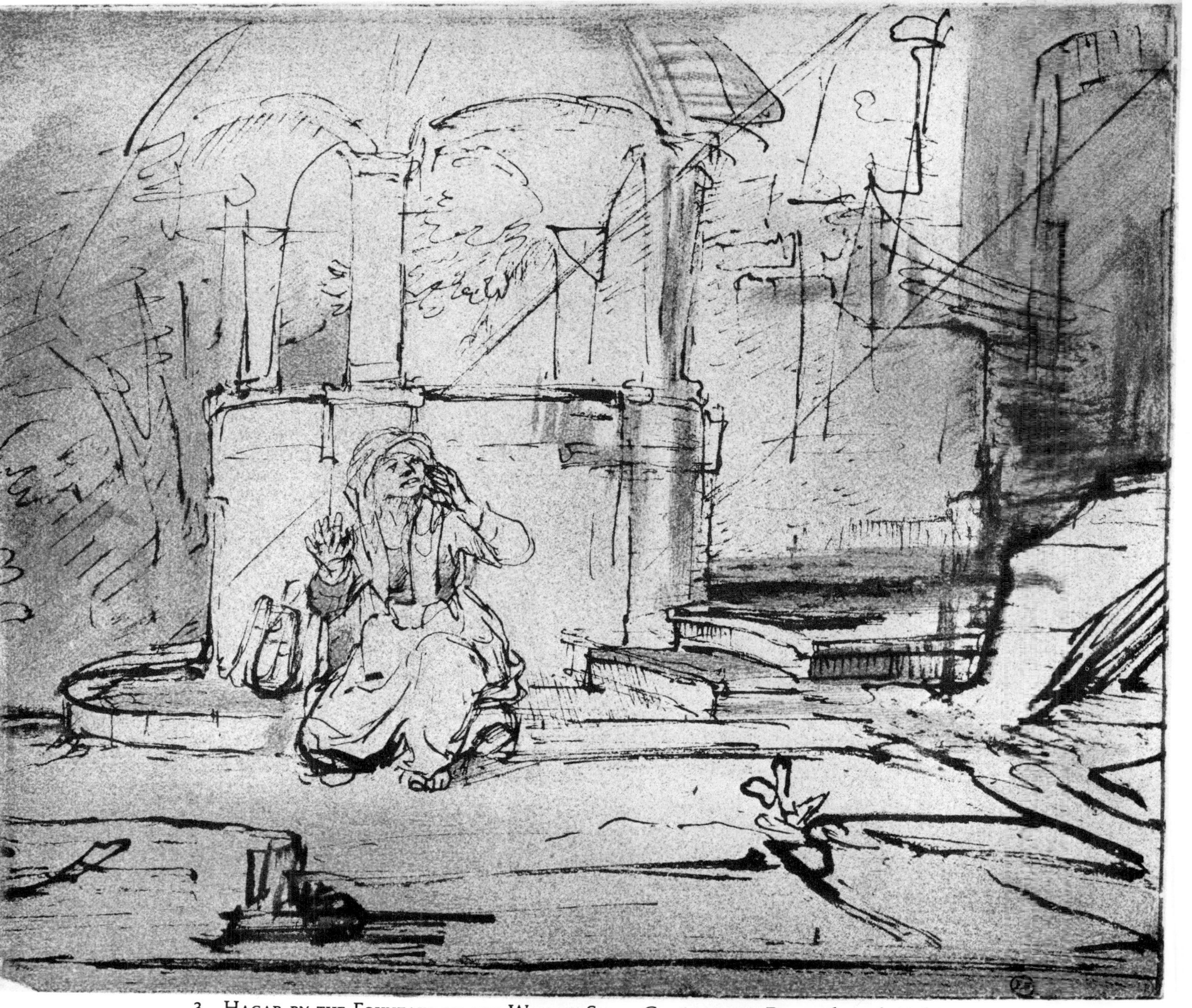

3. Hagar by the Fountain on the Way to Shur. Ca. 1642–45. Pen and wash in bistre, white body color. 191 x 227 mm. Louvre, Paris.

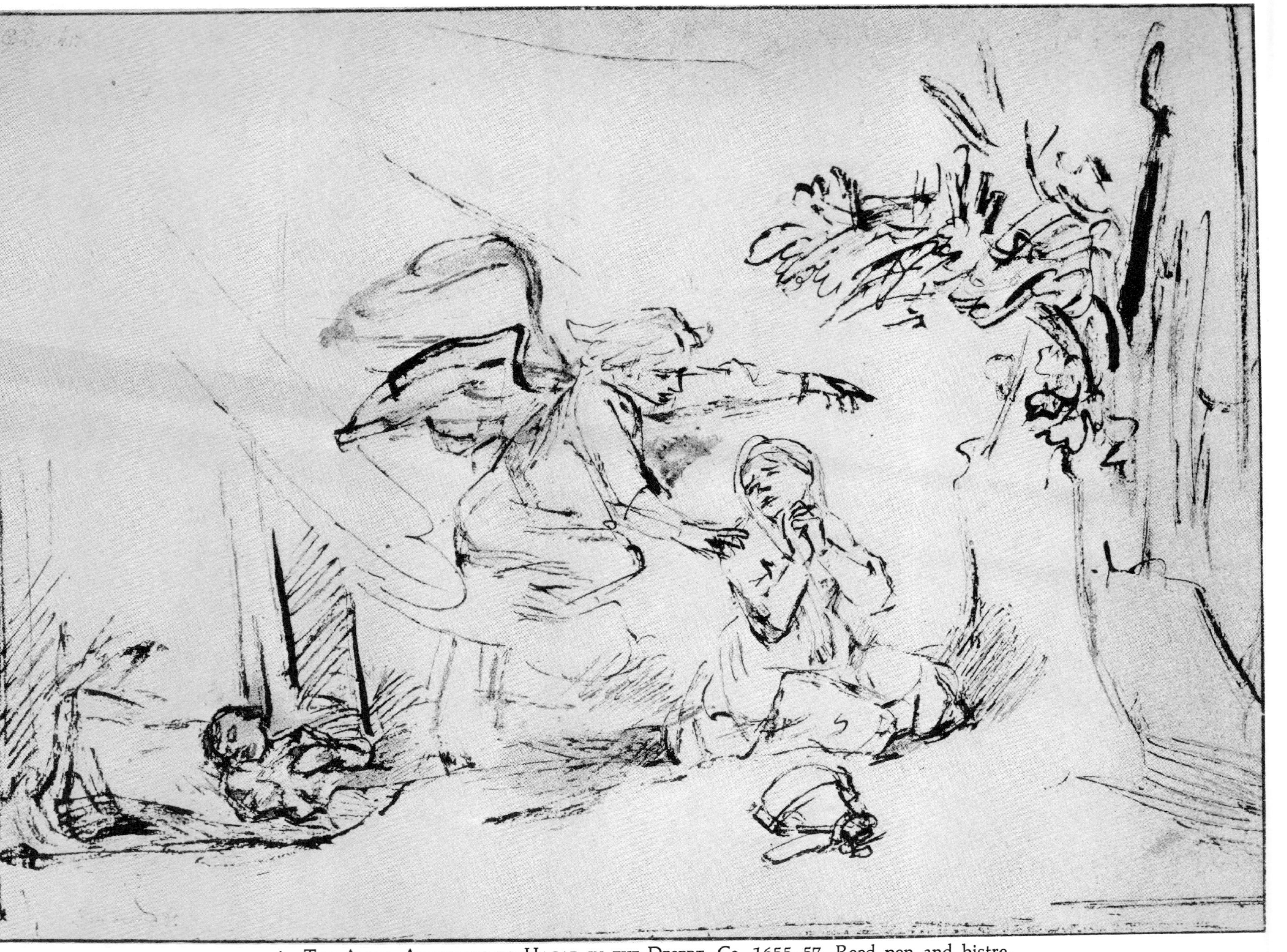

4. THE ANGEL APPEARING TO HAGAR IN THE DESERT. Ca. 1655–57. Reed pen and bistre, white body color. 182 x 252 mm. Kunsthalle, Hamburg.

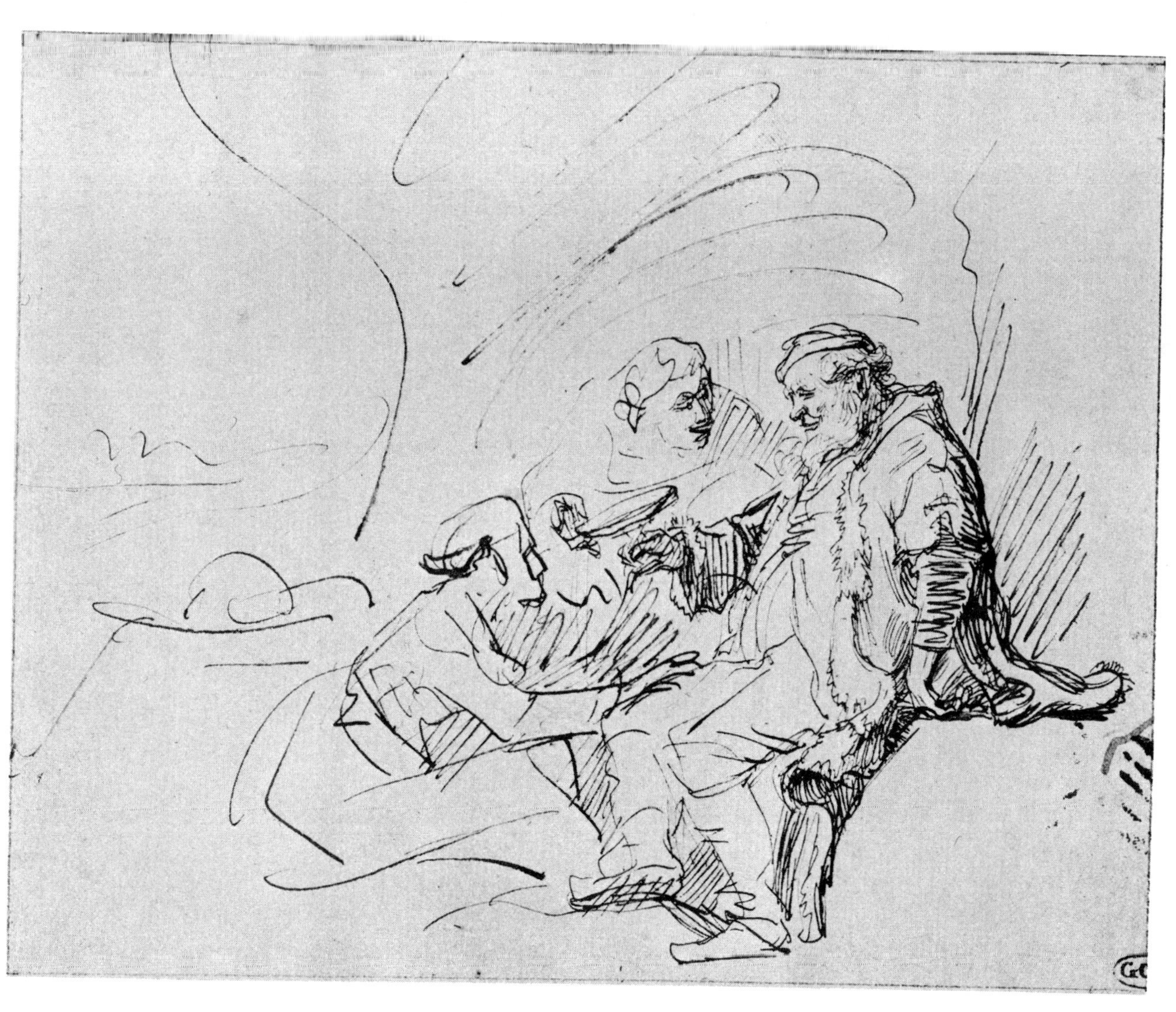

5. Lot and His Daughters. Ca. 1635. Pen and bistre. 152 x 191 mm. Goethe National Museum, Weimar.

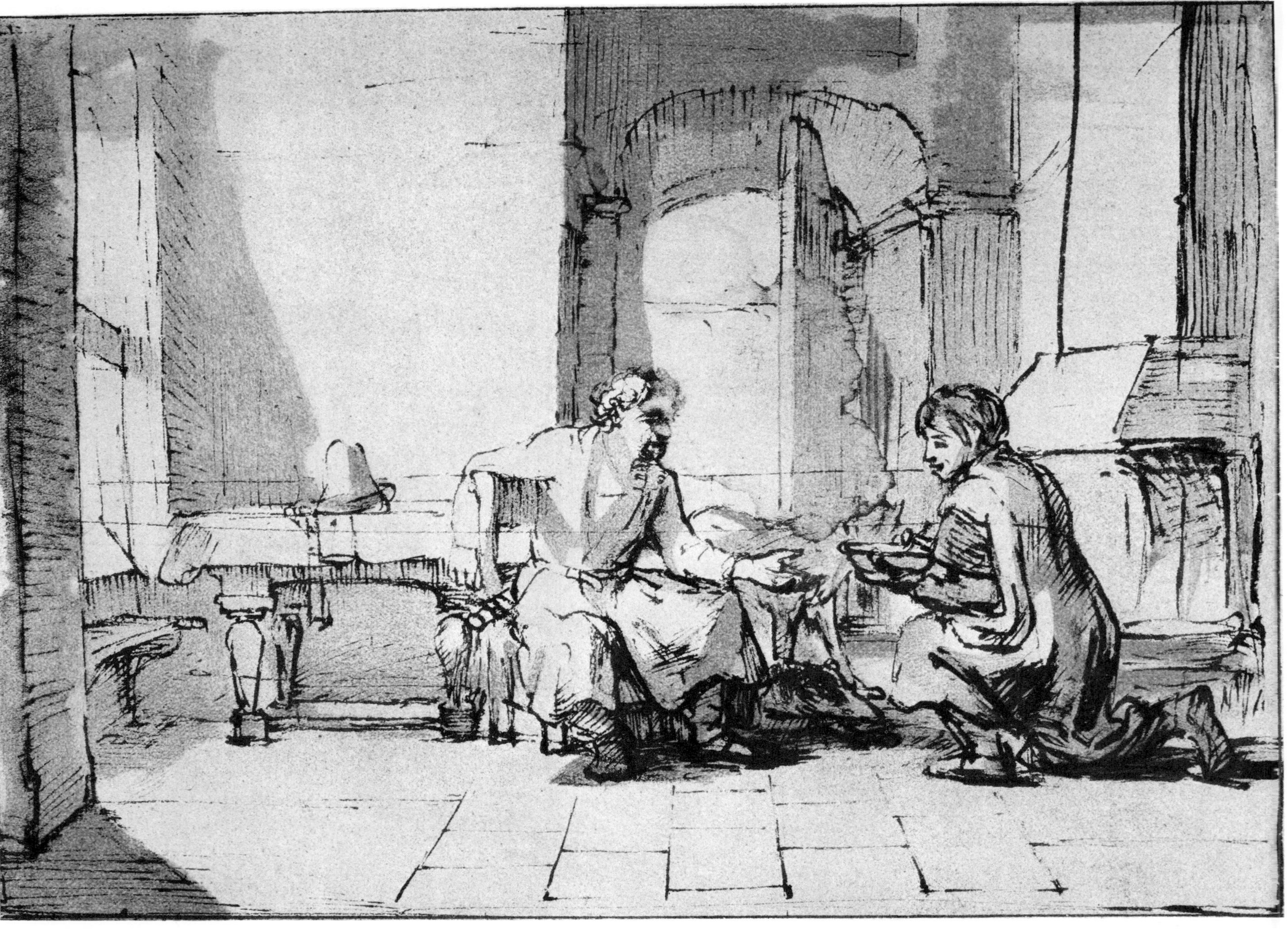

6. Esau Selling His Birthright to Jacob. Ca. 1650. Pen and bistre, wash. 190 x 265 mm. Rembrandt Huis, Amsterdam.

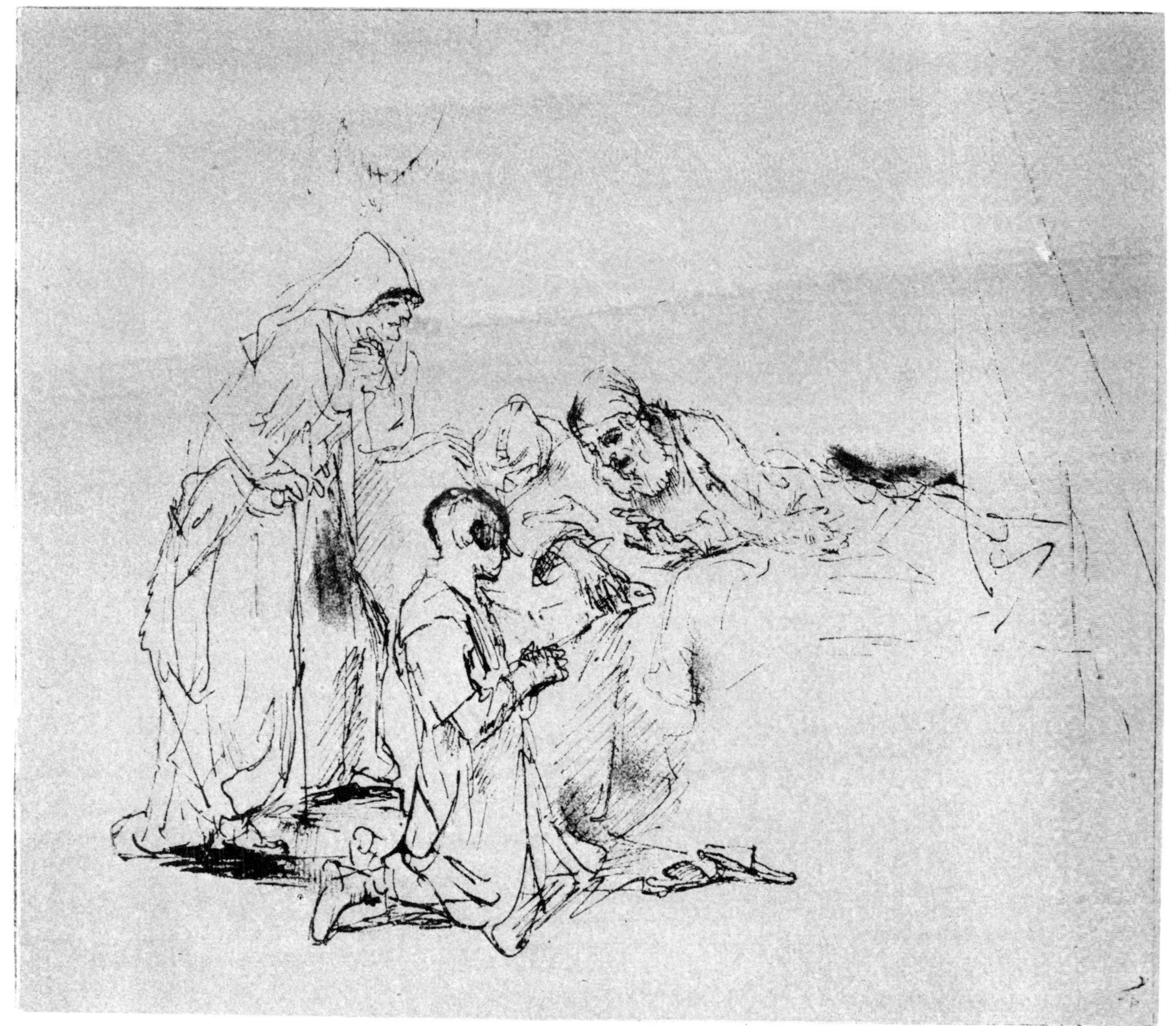

7. Isaac Blessing Jacob. Ca. 1652. Pen and bistre. 175 x 201 mm. Chatsworth Settlement.

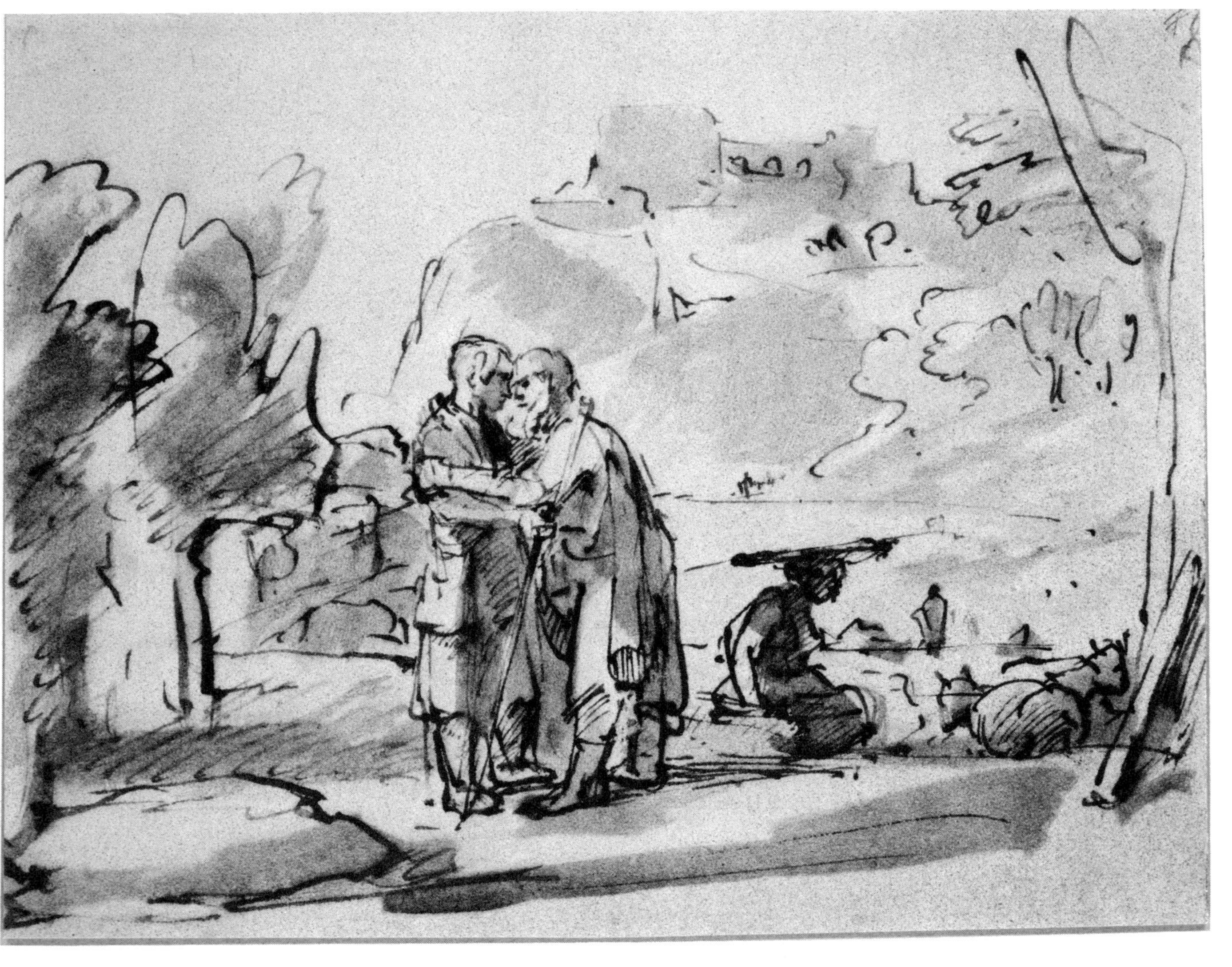

8. The Meeting of Jacob and Laban. Ca. 1652–55. Pen and wash in bistre and Indian ink. 169 x 215 mm. Kobberstiksamling, Copenhagen.

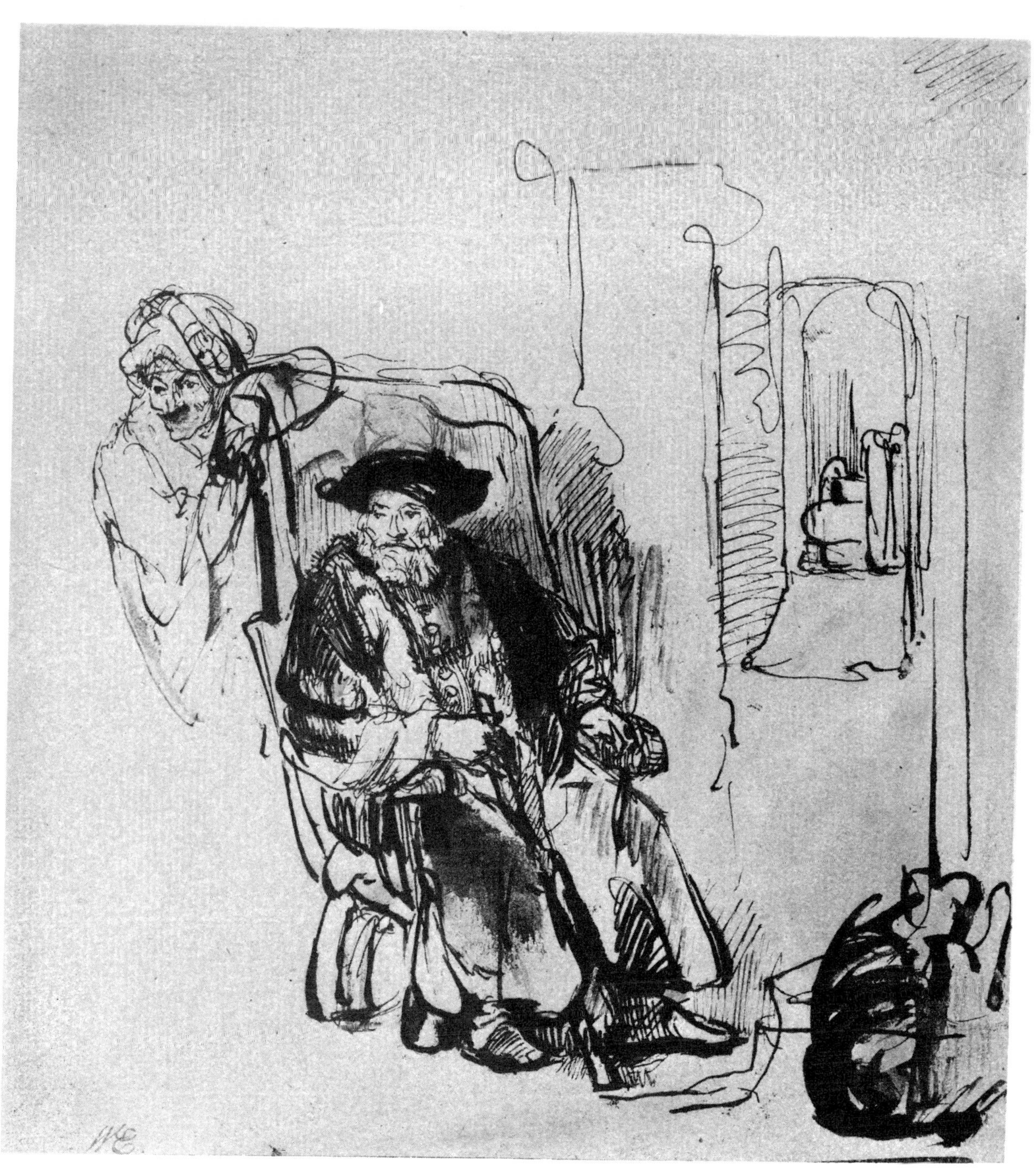

9. Jacob and Rachel Listening to the Account of Joseph's Dreams. Ca. 1638. Pen and wash in bistre, touched with white body color. 180 x 163 mm. British Museum, London.

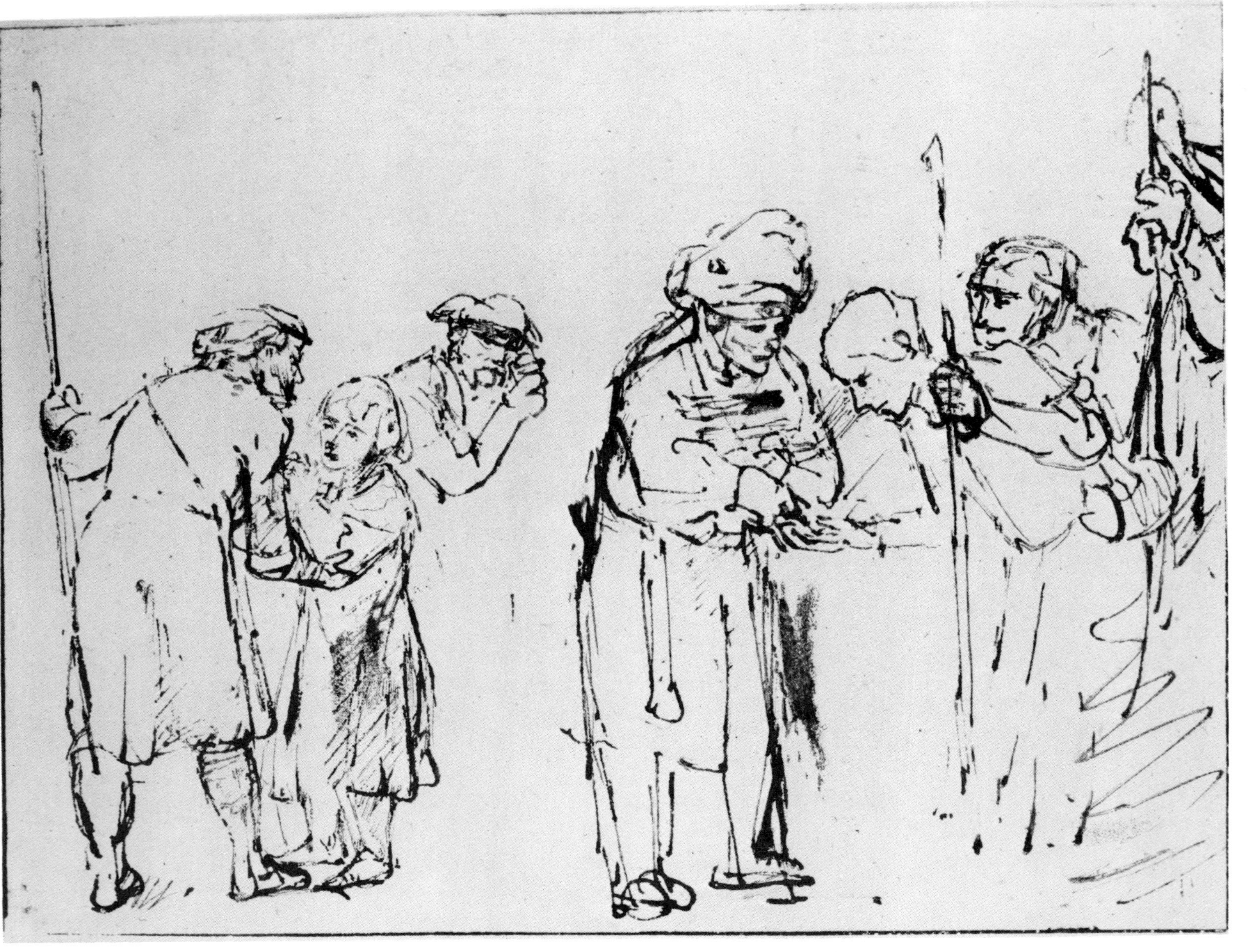

10. Joseph Sold to the Ishmaelites by His Brothers. Ca. 1651–52. Pen and bistre, in some places heightened with white. 158 x 205 mm. Kupferstichkabinett, Berlin.

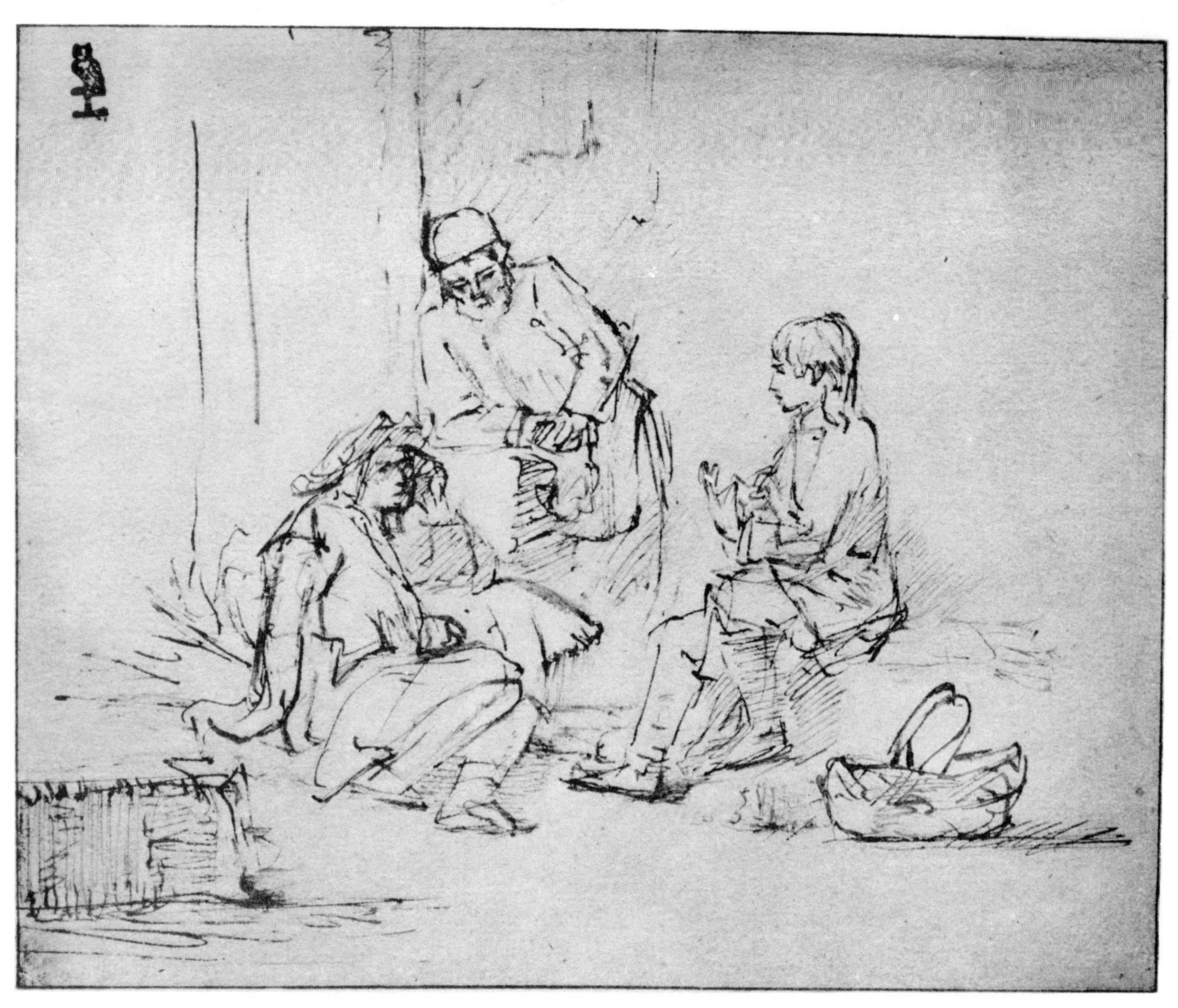

11. Joseph Interpreting the Prisoners' Dreams. Ca. 1652. Reed pen and bistre. 157 x 189 mm. Rijksprentenkabinet, Amsterdam.

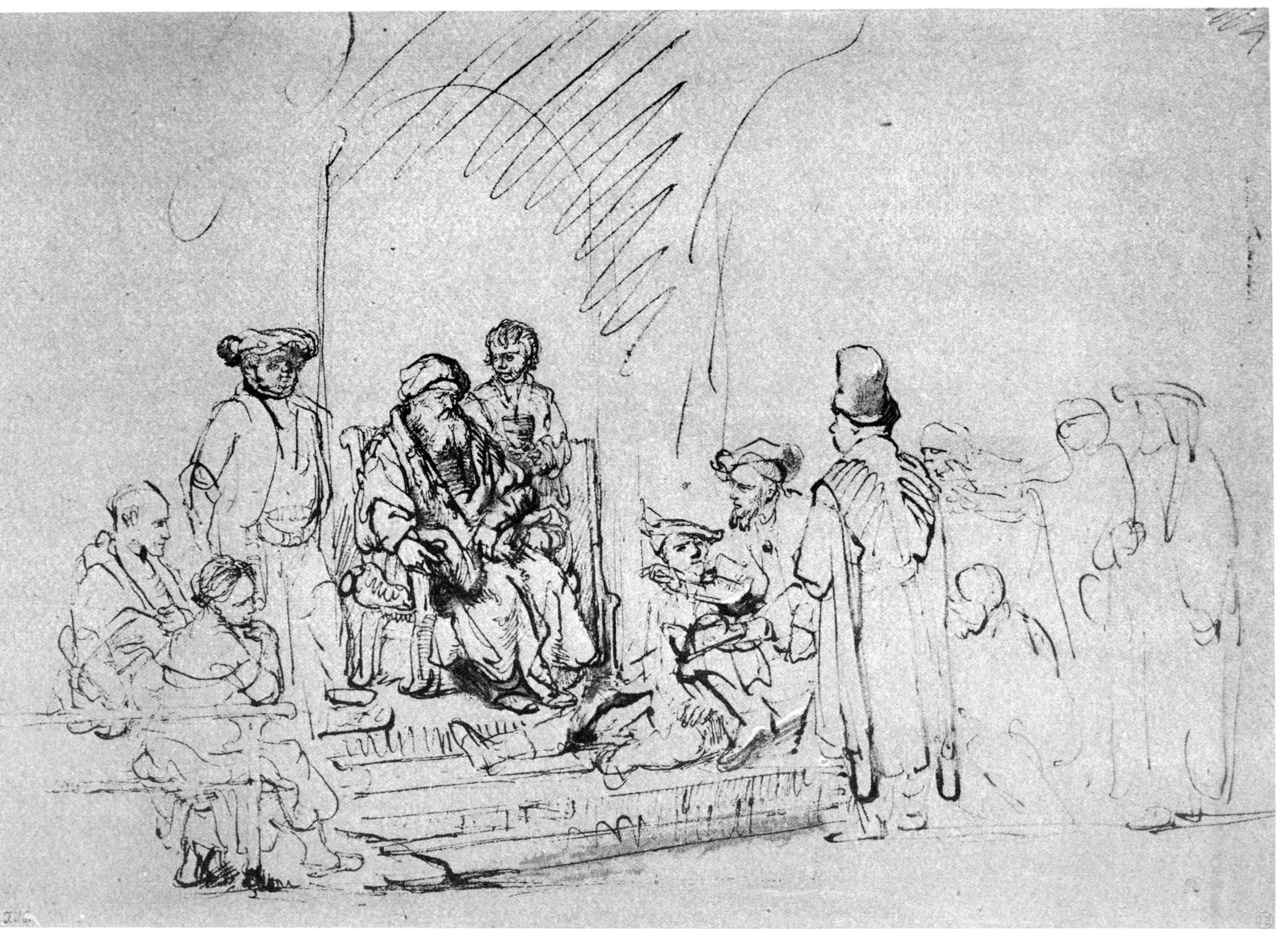

12. Joseph's Brothers Requesting Benjamin from Their Father. Ca. 1638–40. Pen and brush in bistre. 200 x 277 mm. Louvre, Paris.

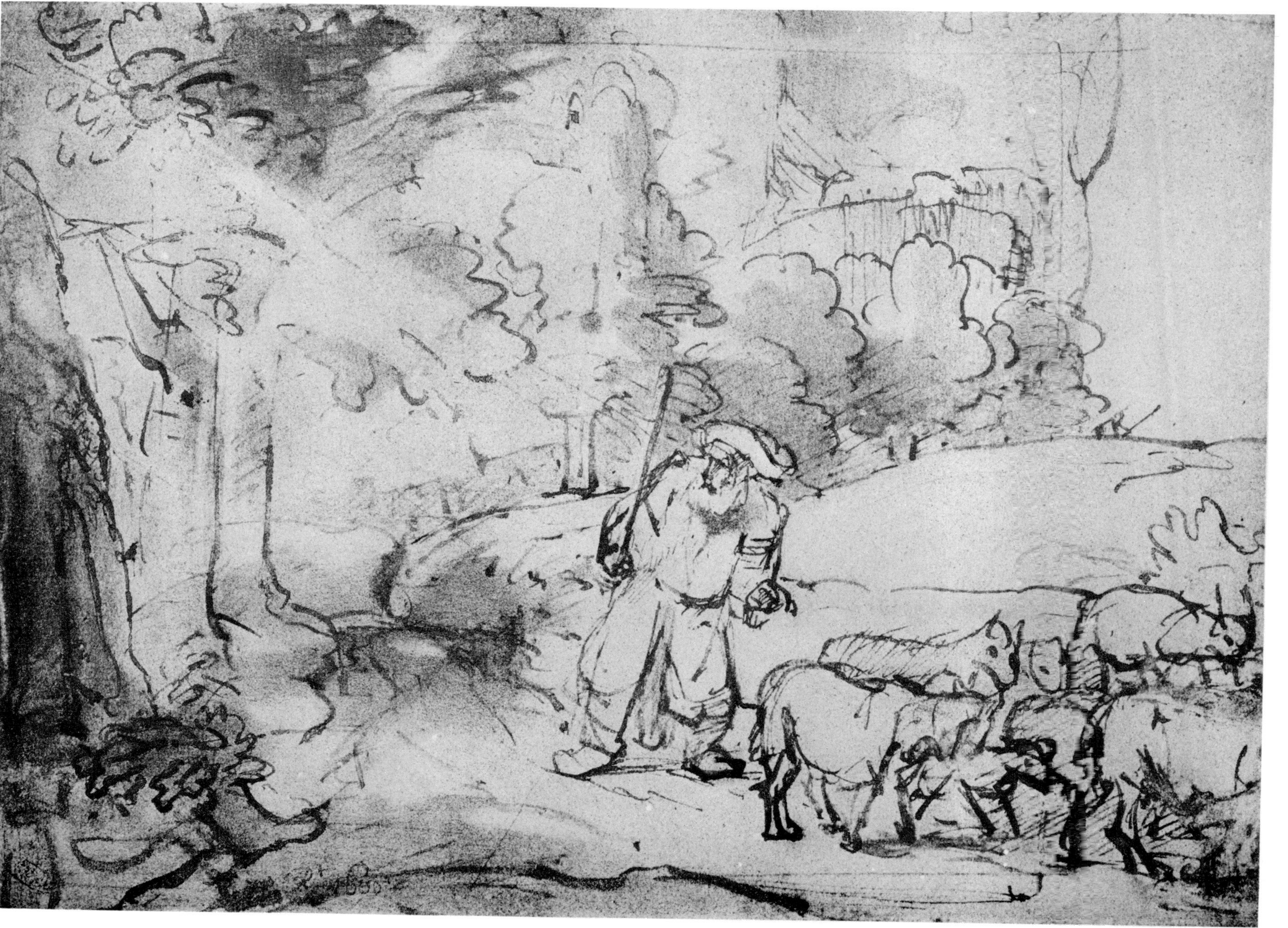

13. Moses and the Burning Bush. Ca. 1655. Reed pen and wash in bistre, white body color. 175 x 247 mm. Sir Max J. Bonn Collection, London.

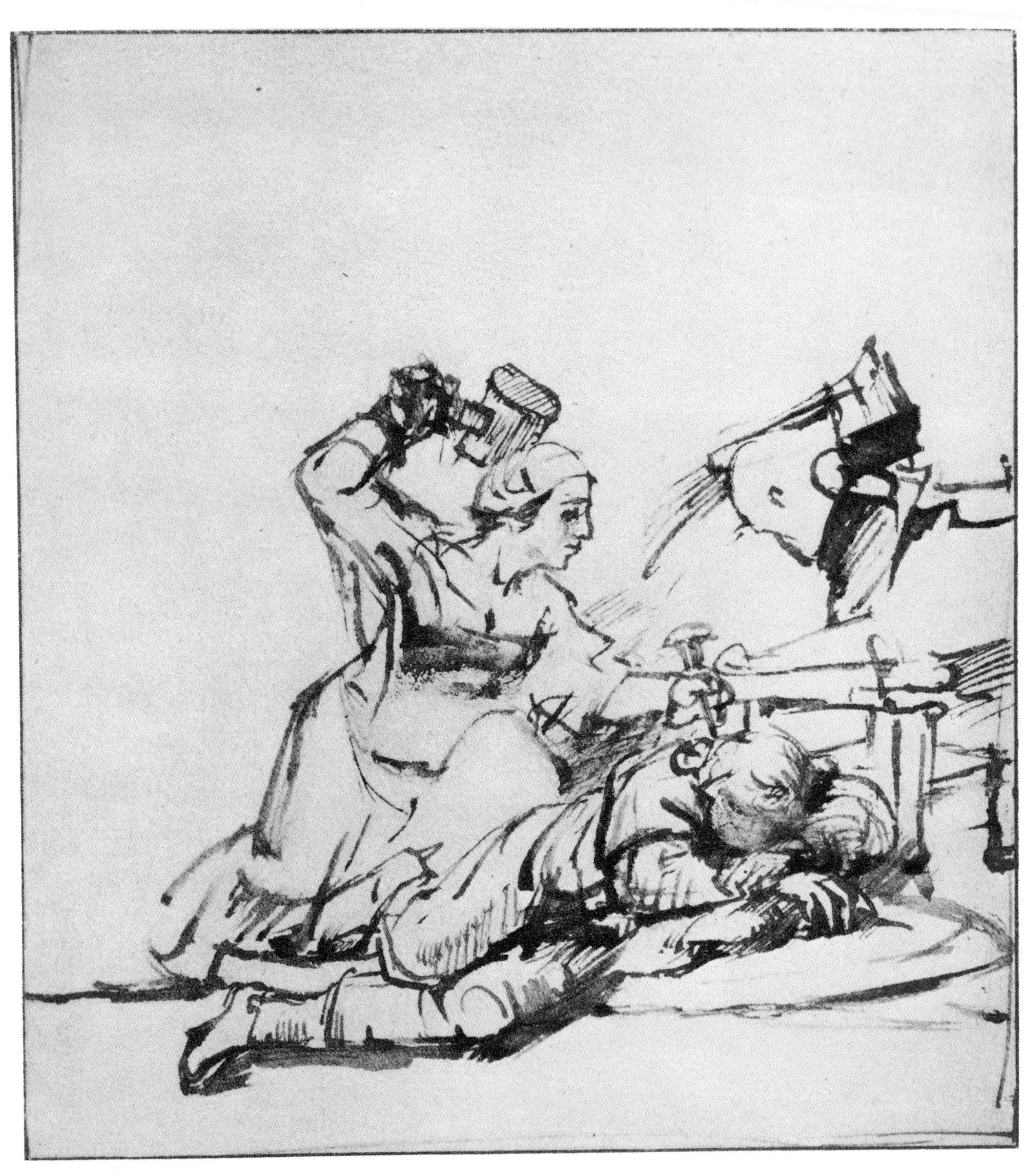

14. Jael Driving a Nail into the Head of Sisera. Ca. 1657–60. Pen and bistre, white body color. 190 x 172 mm. Rijksprentenkabinet, Amsterdam.

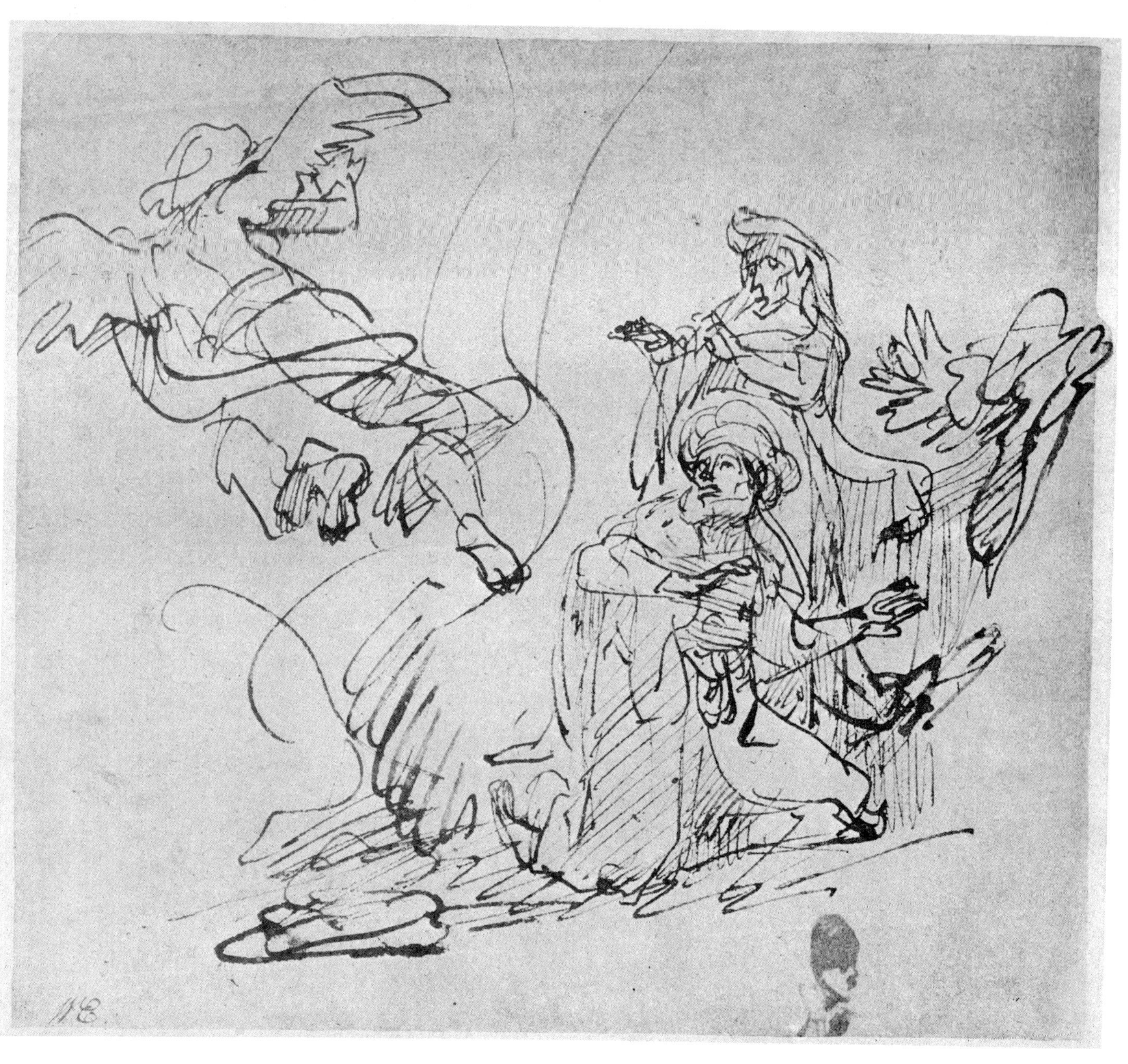

15. The Angel Disappearing After Having Announced to Manoah and His Wife the Birth of Samson. Ca. 1637–40. Pen and bistre. 175 x 190 mm. Kupferstichkabinett, Berlin.

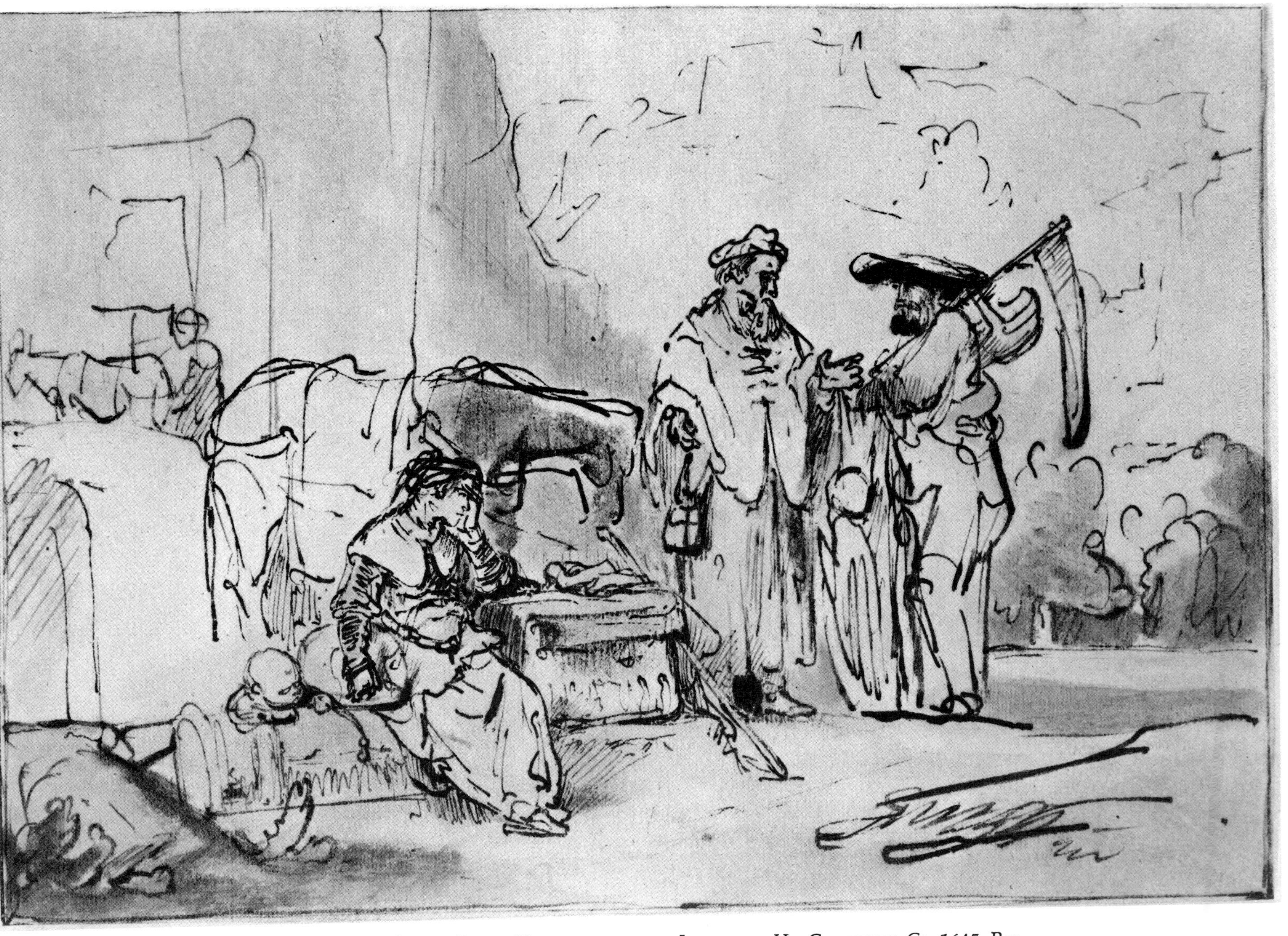

16. A Man of Gibeah Offers Hospitality to the Levite and His Concubine. Ca. 1645. Pen and wash in bistre. 180 x 246 mm. British Museum, London.

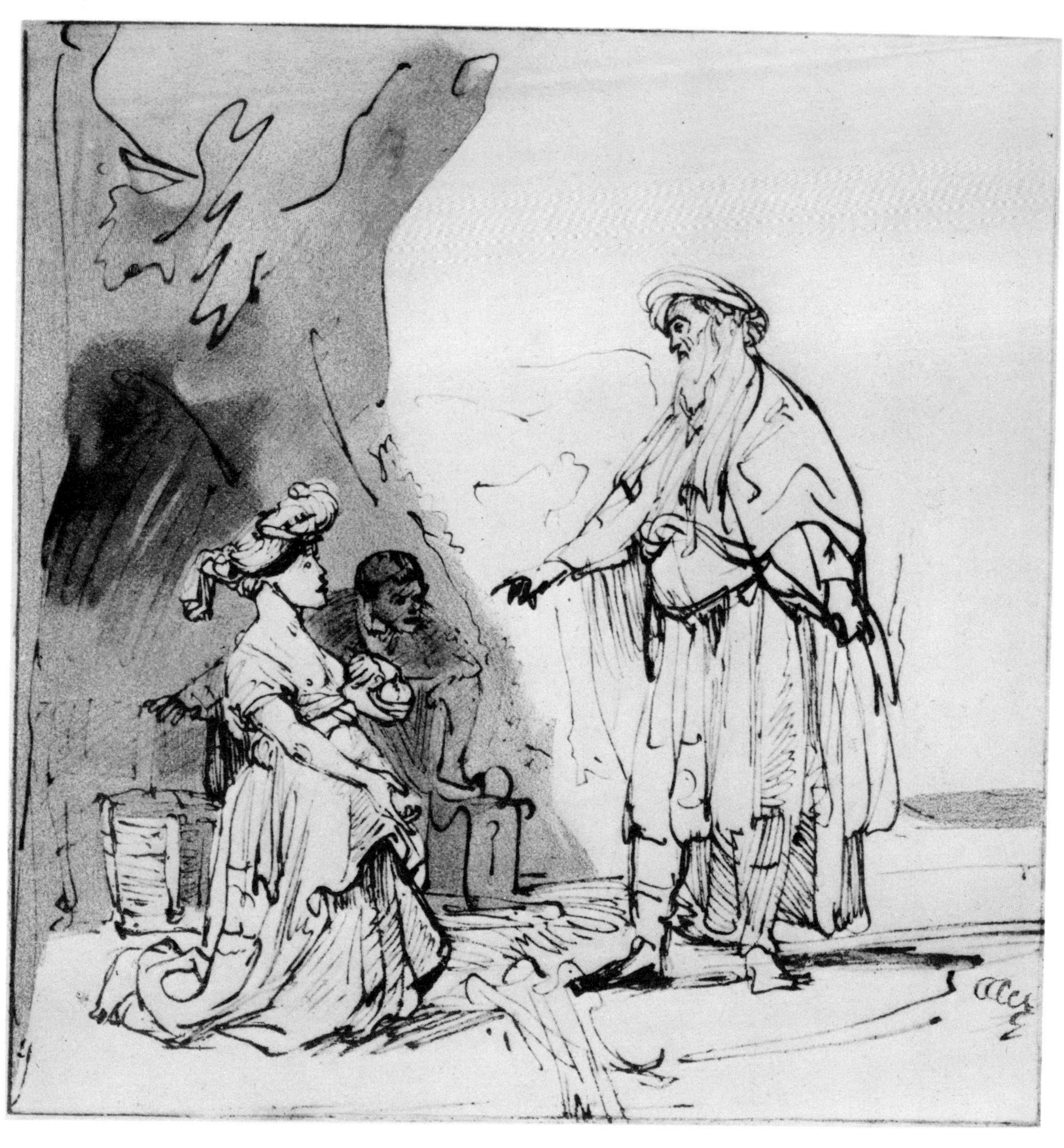

17. Boaz and Ruth in the Field. Ca. 1638. Pen and bistre. 178 x 169 mm. Kupferstichkabinett, Berlin.

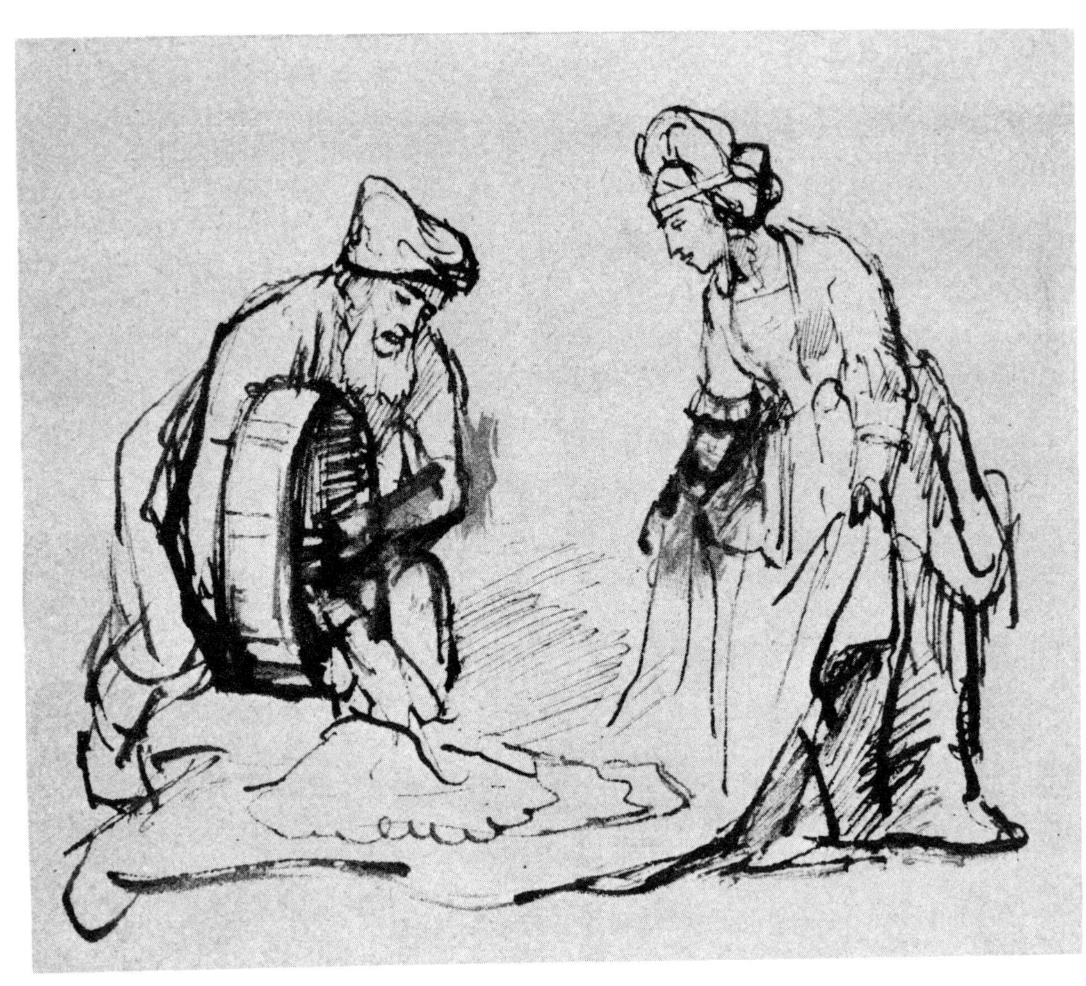

18. Boaz Pours Six Measures of Barley into Ruth's Veil. Ca. 1648–50. Pen and bistre, white body color. 126 x 143 mm. Rijksprentenkabinet, Amsterdam.

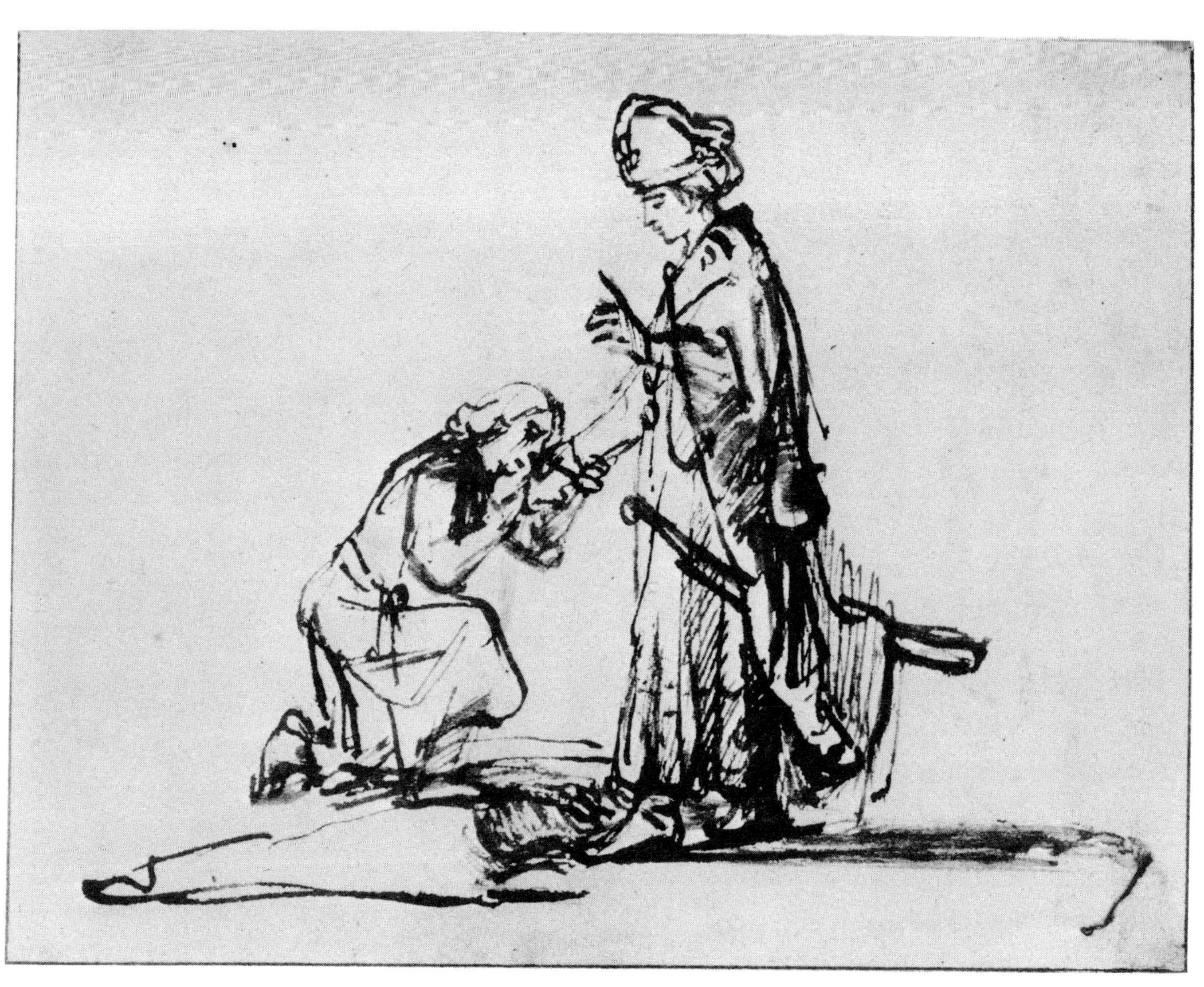

19. David Taking Leave of Jonathan. Ca. 1655–58. Pen and bistre. 143 x 183 mm. Rijksprentenkabinet, Amsterdam.

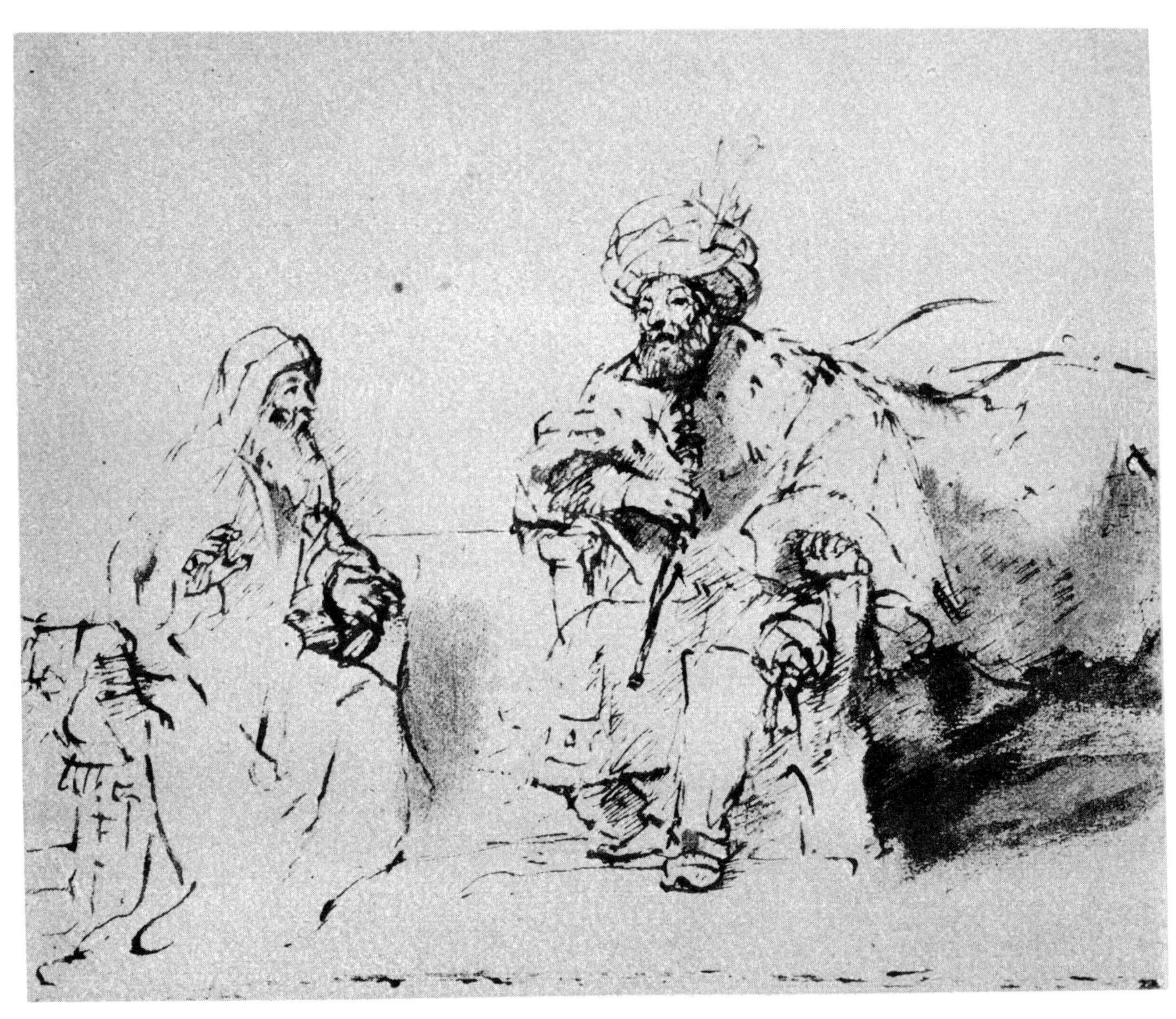

20. Nathan Admonishing David. Ca. 1655. Reed pen and wash in bistre. 146 x 173 mm. Kupferstichkabinett, Berlin.

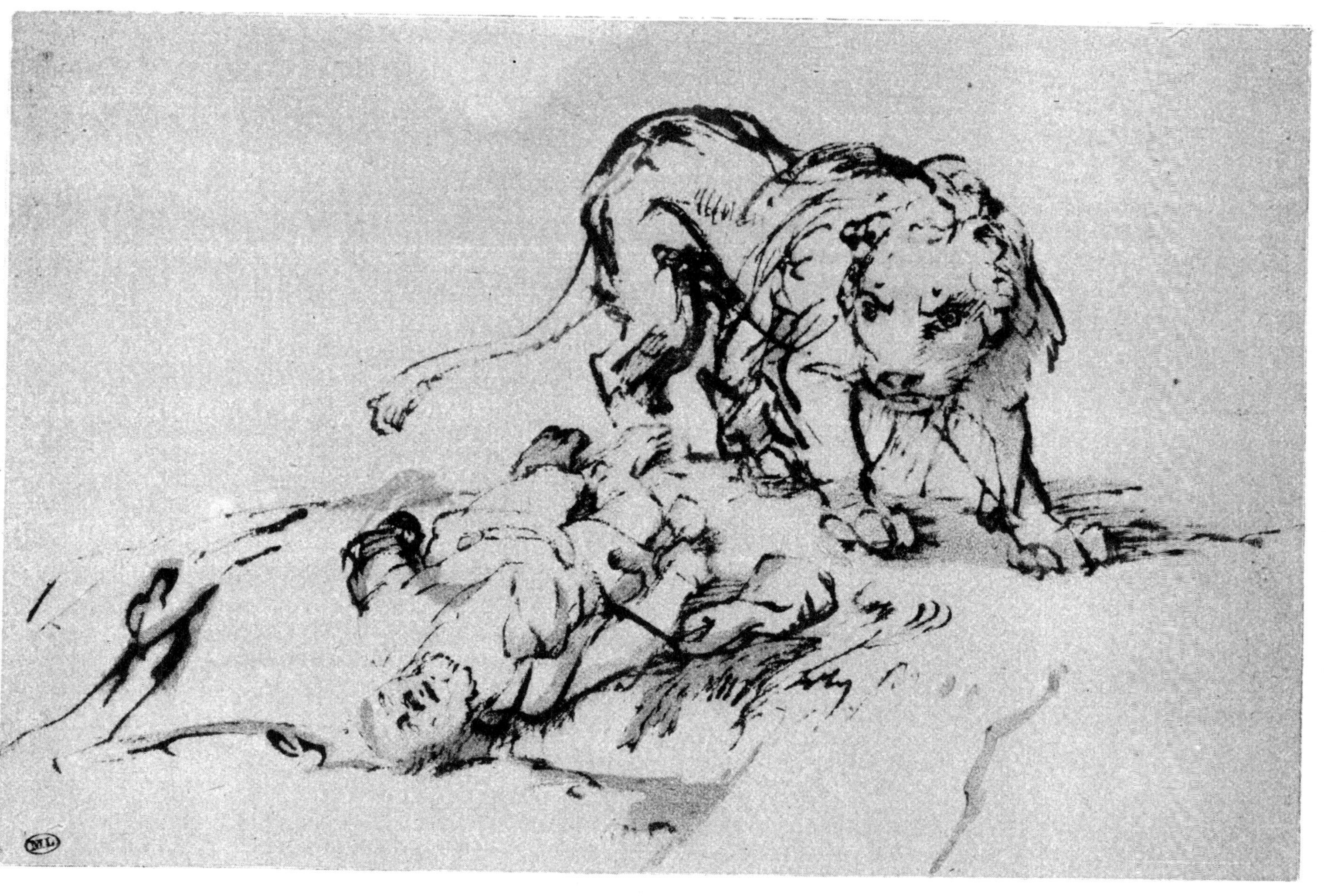

21. The Lion by the Body of the Disobedient Prophet. Ca. 1655. Reed pen and bistre, white body color. 137 x 205 mm. Louvre, Paris.

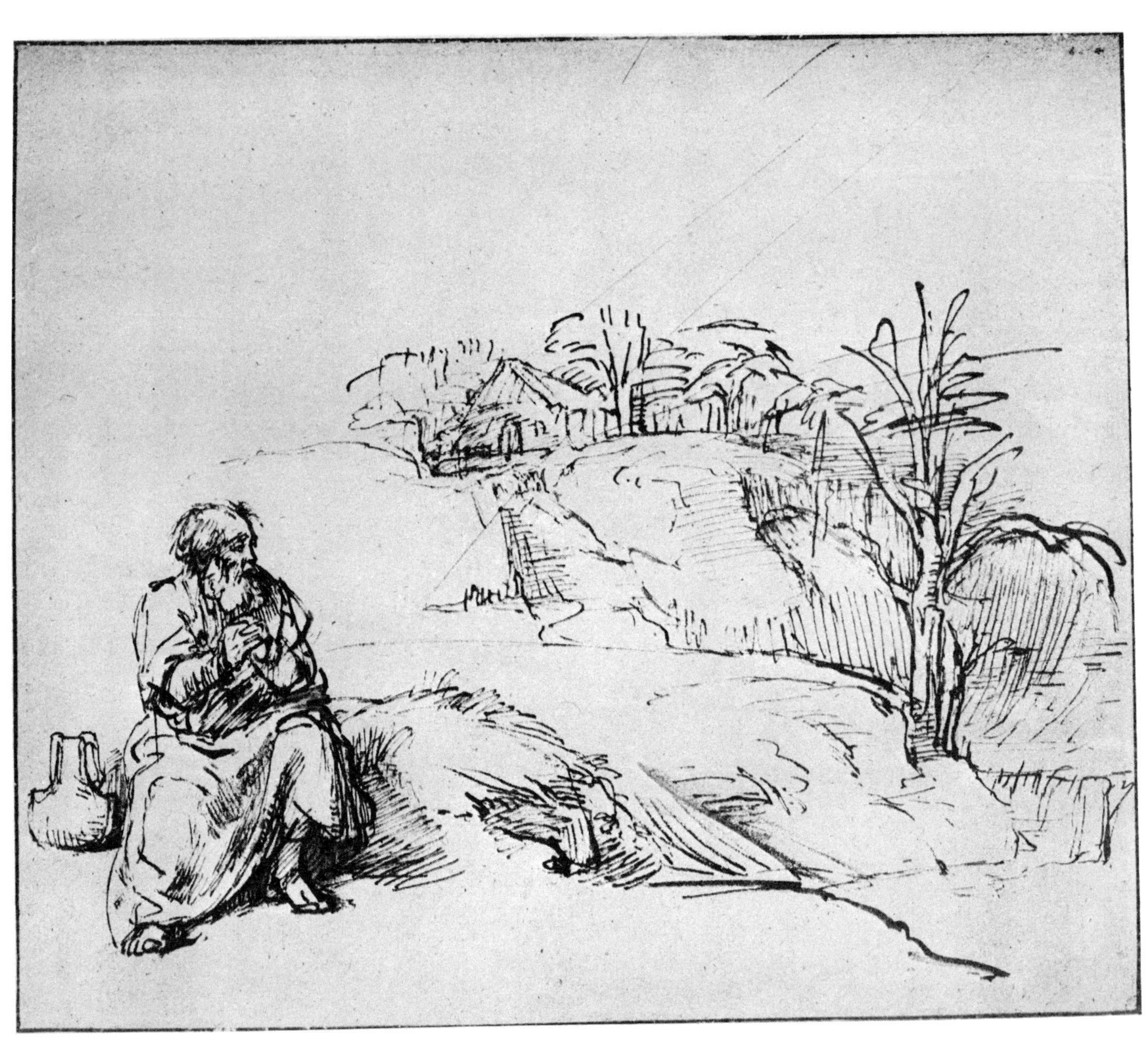

22. THE PROPHET ELIJAH BY THE BROOK CHERITH. Ca. 1655. Reed pen and bistre, wash, white body color. 205 x 233 mm. Kupferstichkabinett, Berlin.

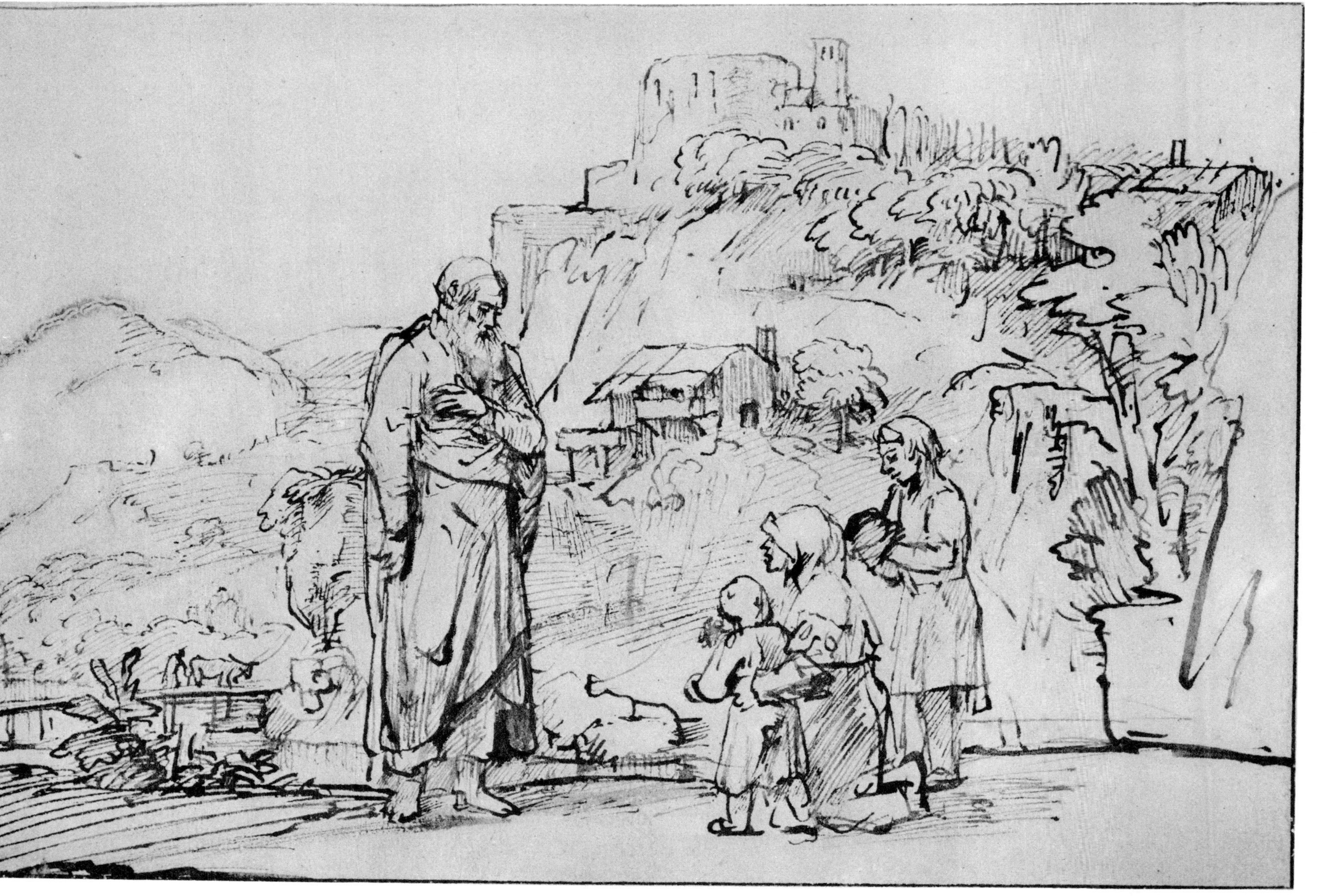

23. The Prophet Elisha and the Widow with Her Sons. Ca. 1657. Pen and bistre. 172 x 254 mm. Dr. Felix Somary, Washington, D.C.

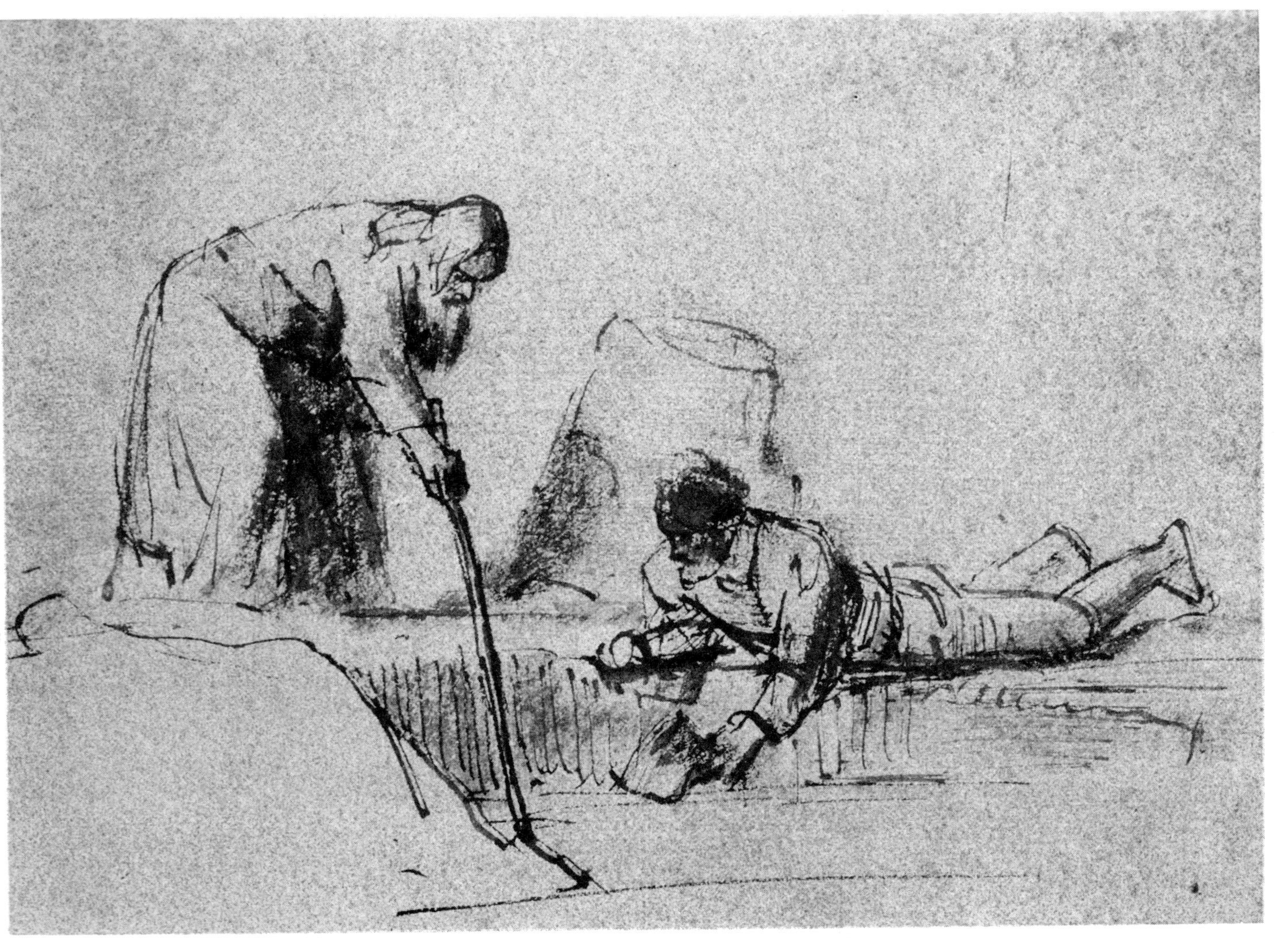

24. The Miracle of Elisha Making a Piece of Iron Float on Water. Ca. 1650–53. Pen and bistre; wash rubbed with the finger. 140 x 188 mm. Bredius Museum, The Hague.

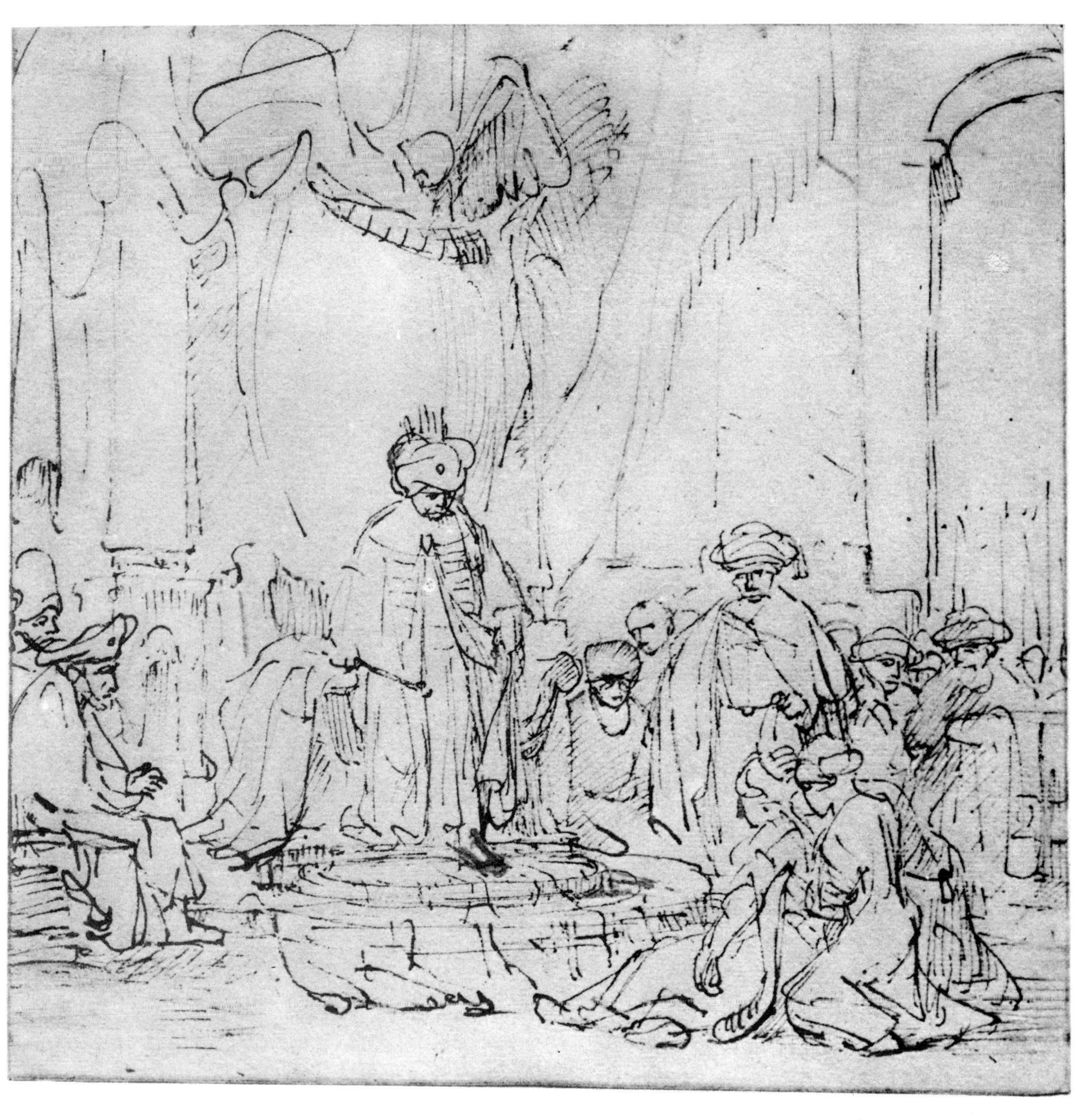

25. Esther Fainting Before Ahasuerus. Ca. 1645–50. Pen and bistre. 175 x 177 mm. Rijksprentenkabinet, Amsterdam.

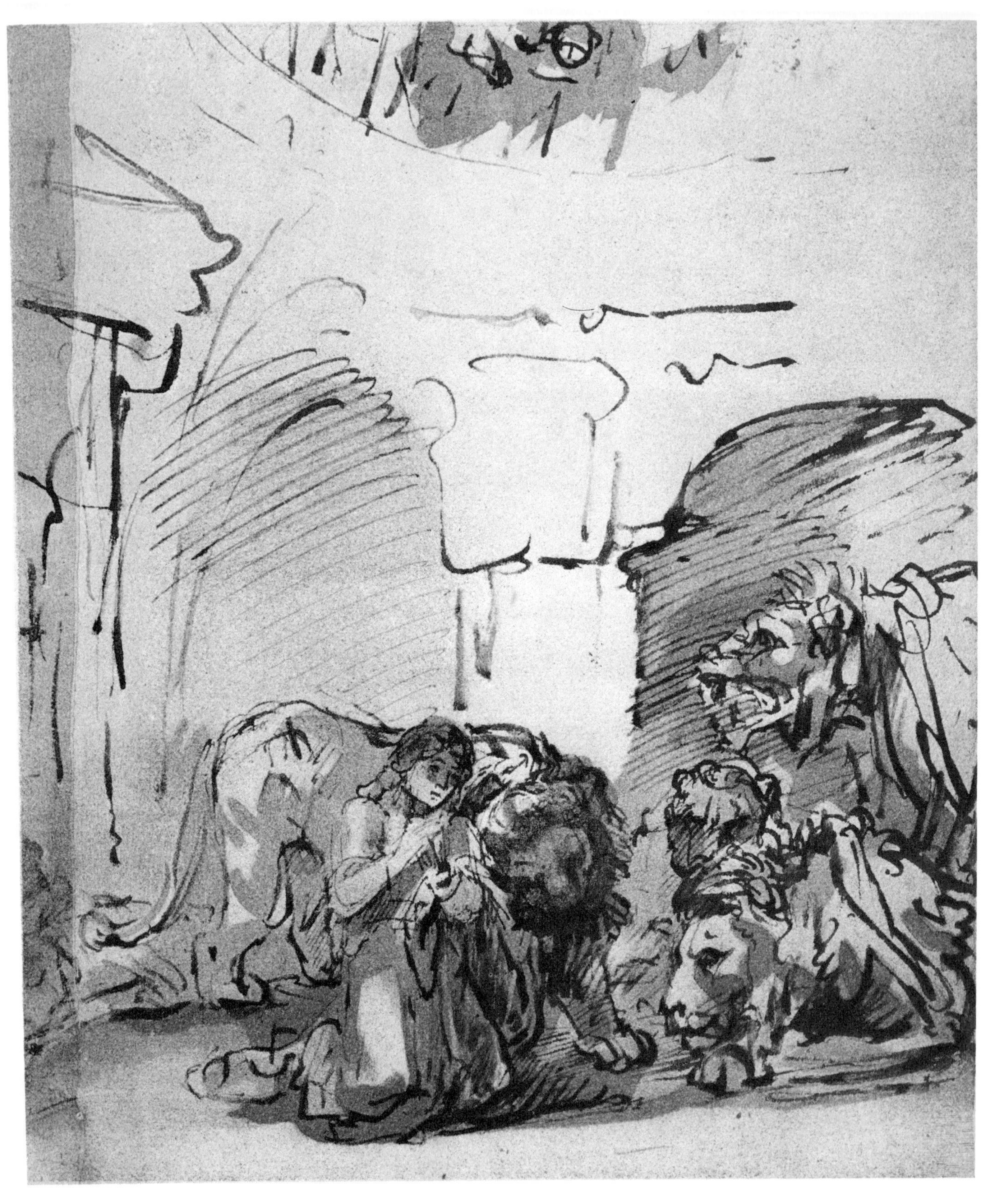

26. Daniel in the Lions' Den. Ca. 1652. Reed pen and bistre, wash, white body color. 222 x 185 mm. Rijksprentenkabinet, Amsterdam.

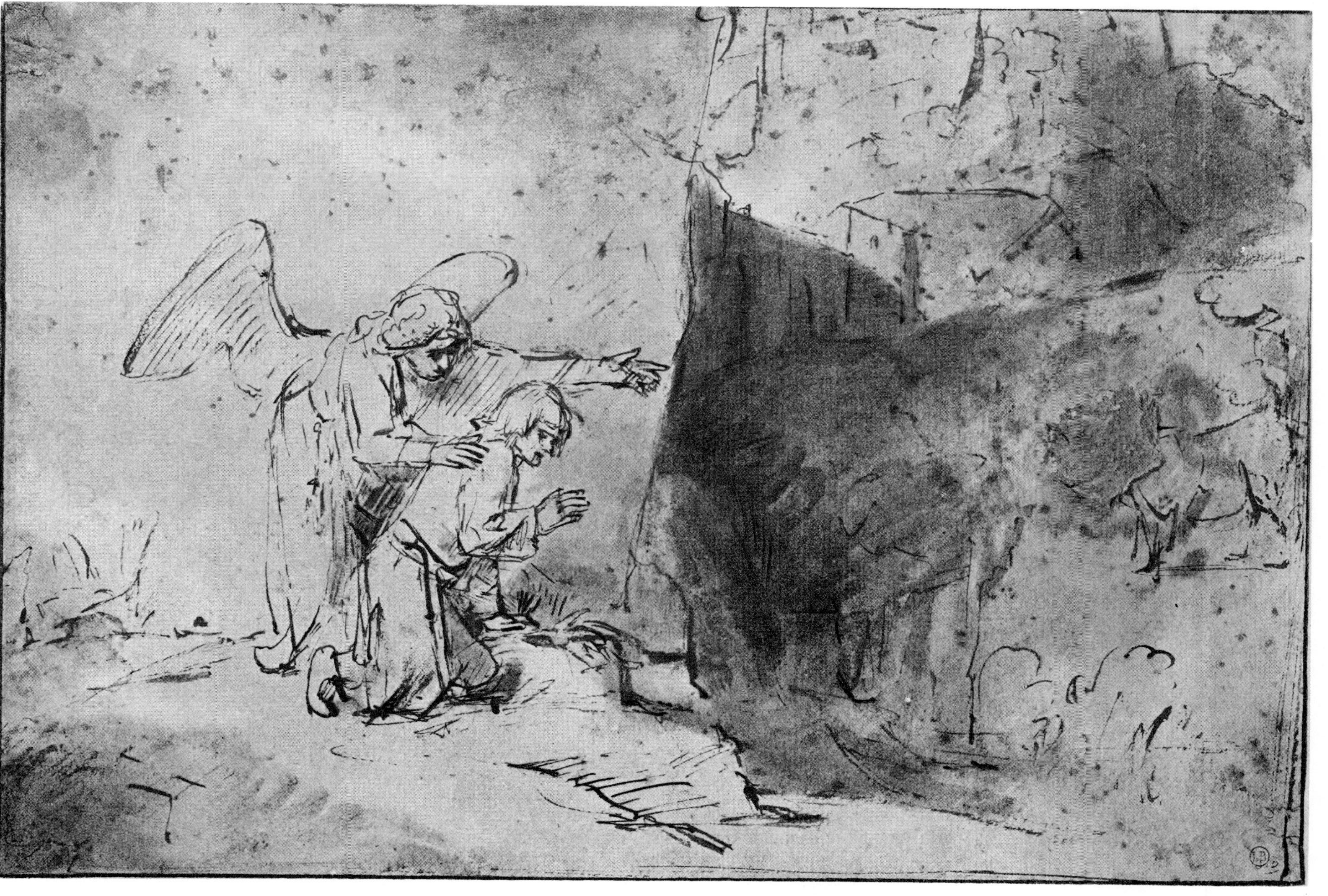

27. The Vision of Daniel. Ca. 1652. Reed pen and wash in bistre. 165 x 243 mm. Louvre, Paris.

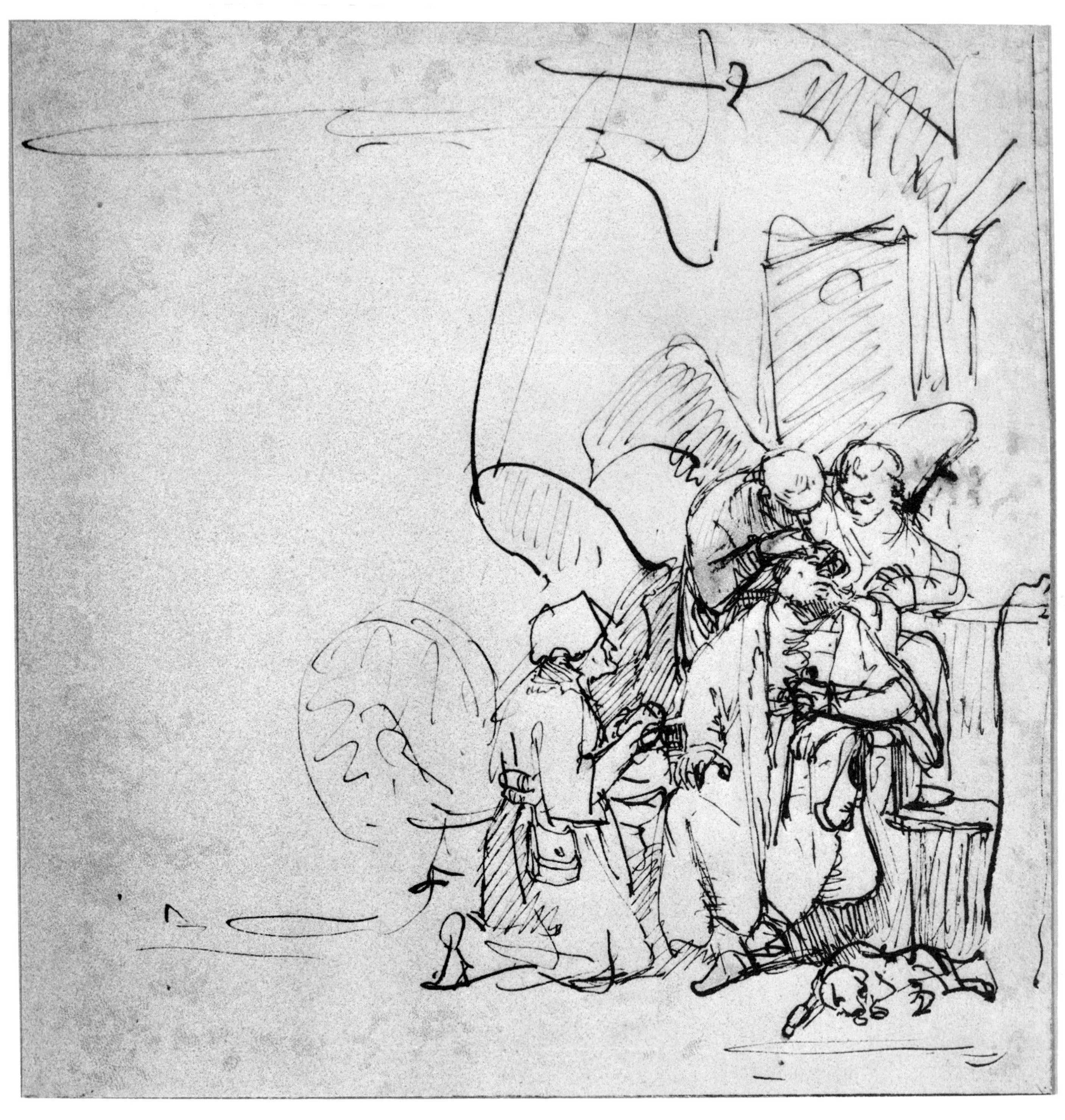

28. The Healing of Tobit. Ca. 1640. Pen and bistre. 207 x 200 mm. Fodor Museum, Amsterdam.

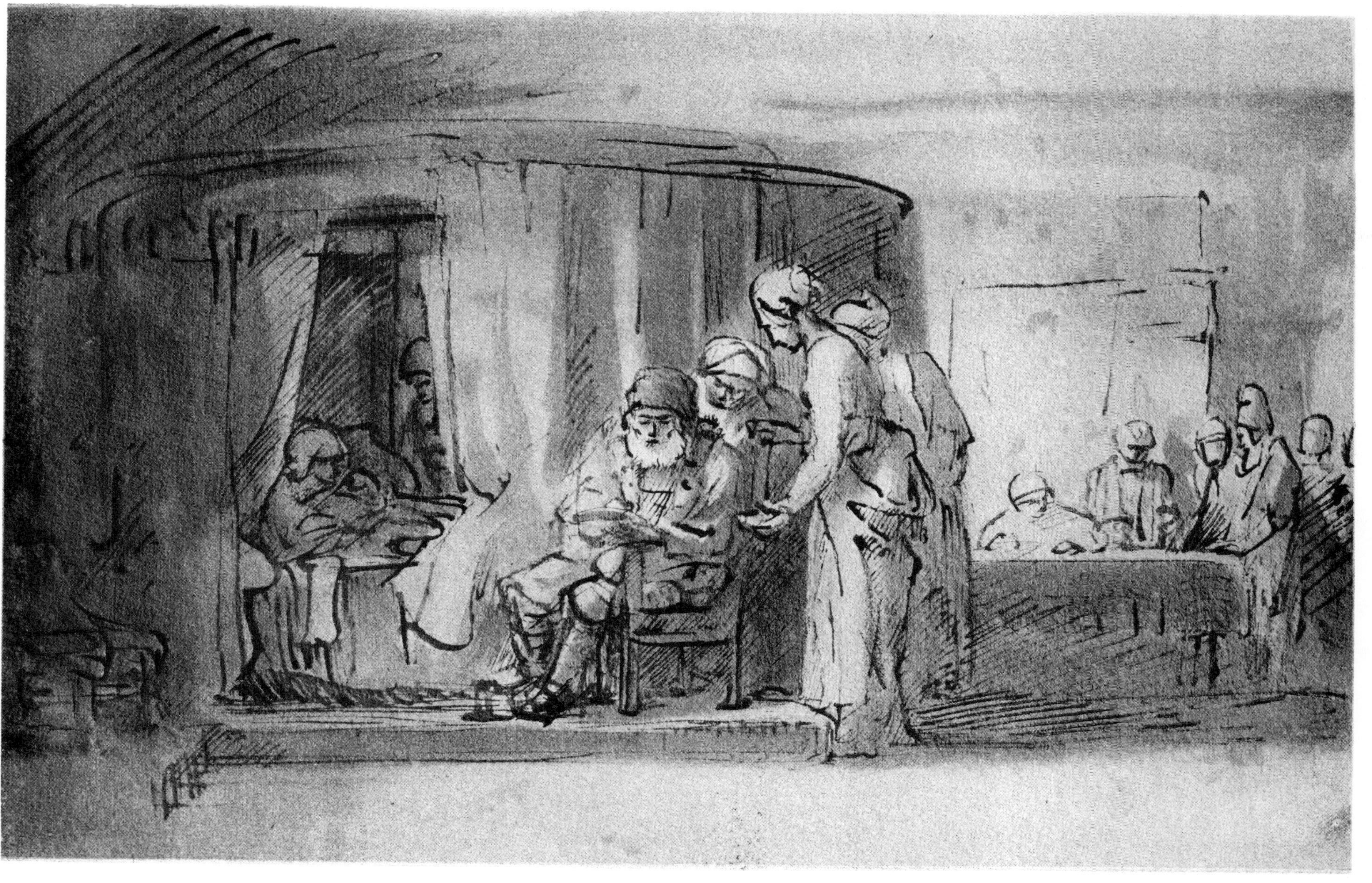

29. The Naming of St. John the Baptist. Ca. 1655. Pen and wash in bistre and Indian ink. 199 x 314 mm. Louvre, Paris.

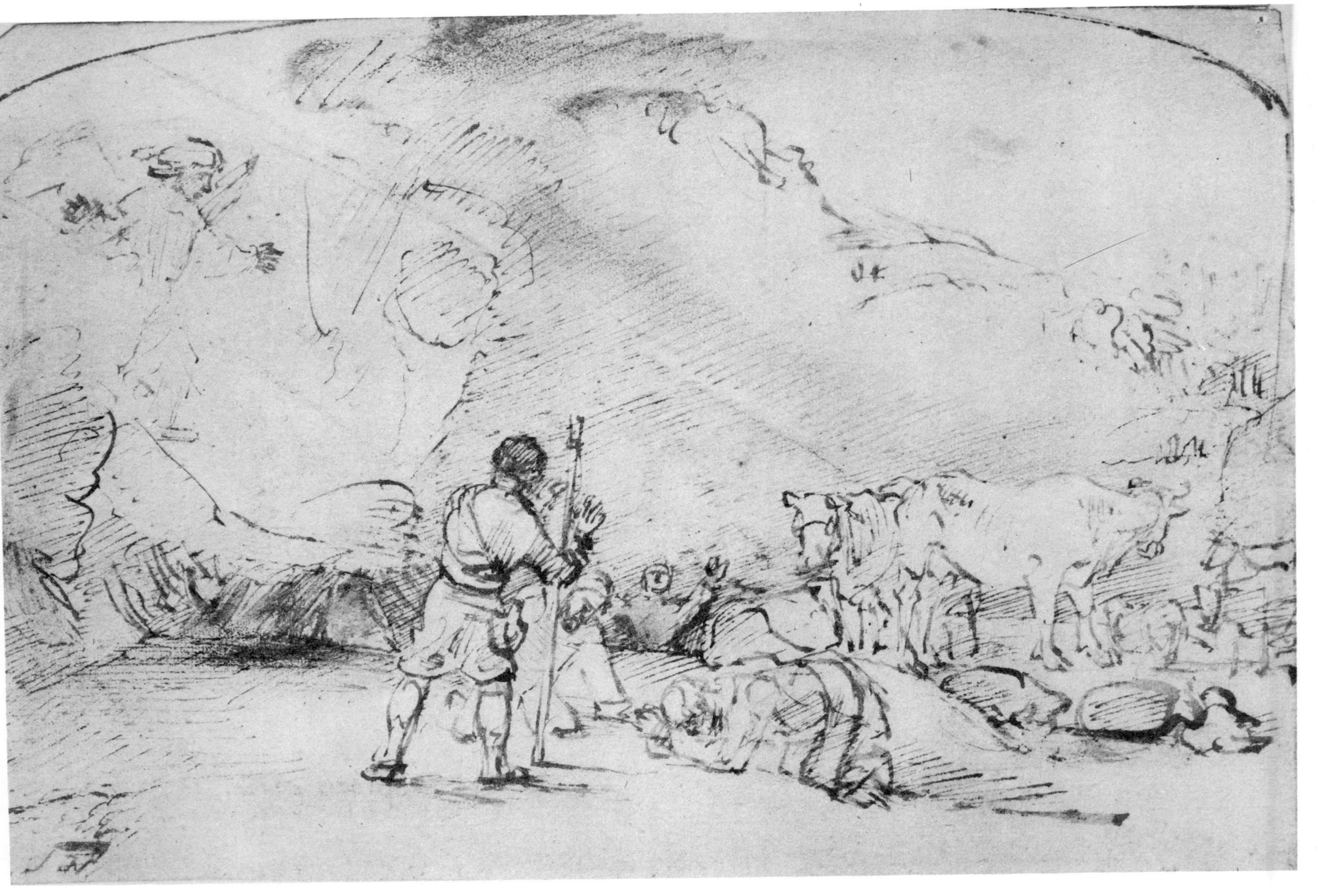

30. The Annunciation to the Shepherds. Ca. 1655. Pen and wash in bistre. 188 x 280 mm. Rijksprentenkabinet, Amsterdam.

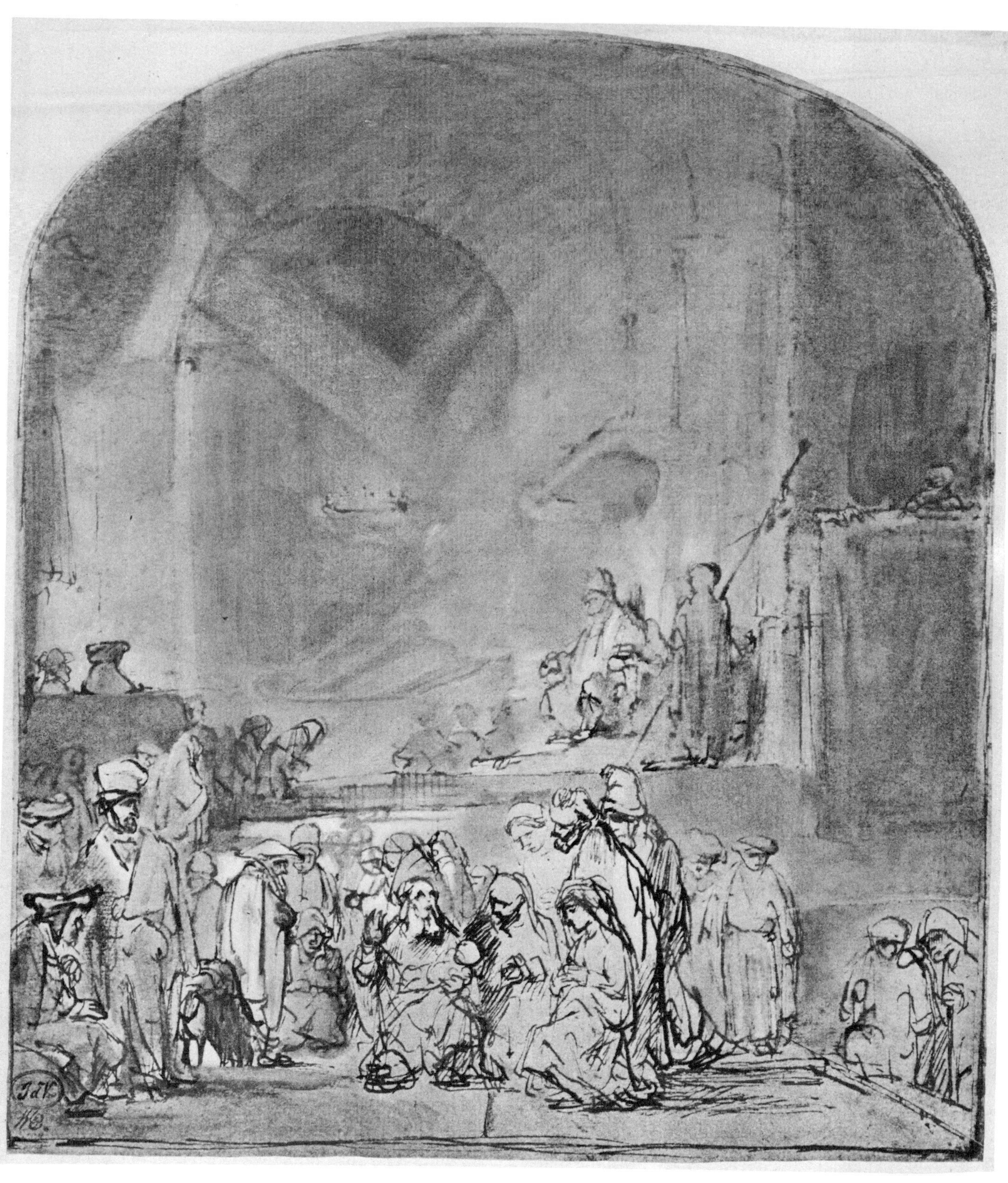

31. The Presentation in the Temple. Ca. 1647. Pen and wash, black chalk, heightened with white. 238 x 208 mm. Louvre, Paris.

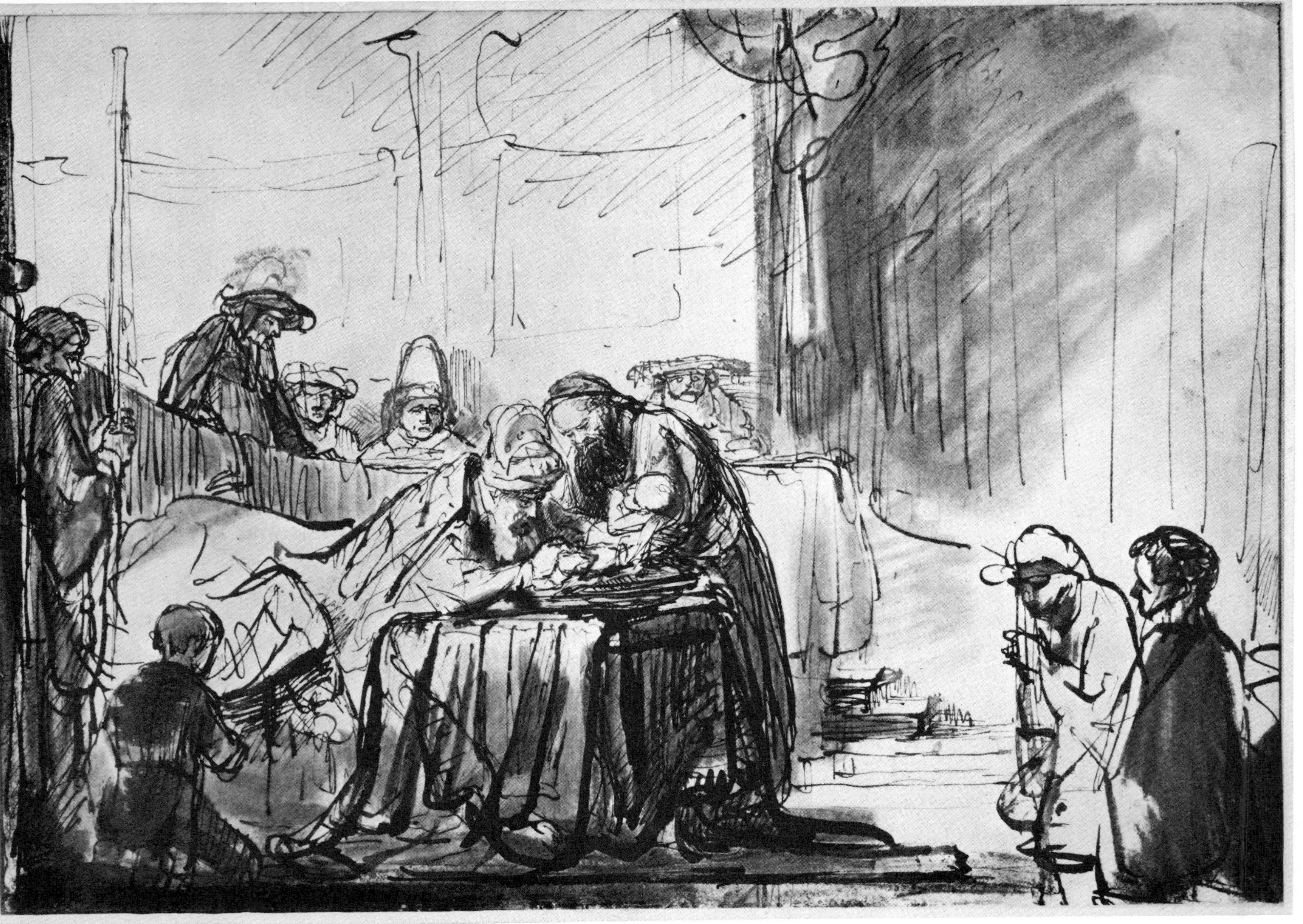

32. The CIRCUMCISION OF CHRIST. Ca. 1645. Pen and bistre, wash, heightened with white. 203 x 287 mm. Kupferstichkabinett, Berlin.

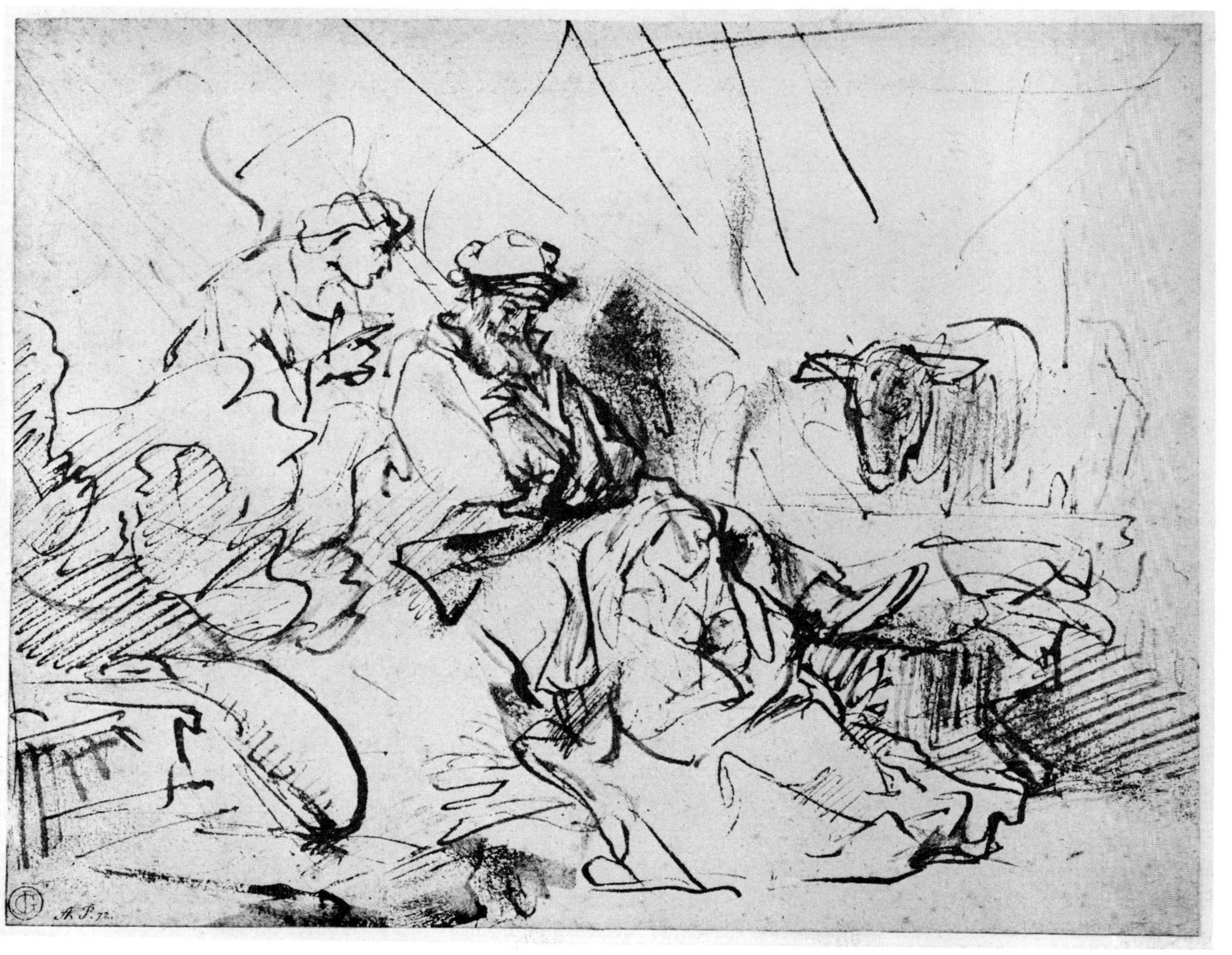

33. The Angel Appearing to Joseph in His Dream. Ca. 1648–50. Pen and bistre, wash, white body color. 145 x 187 mm. Kupferstichkabinett, Berlin.

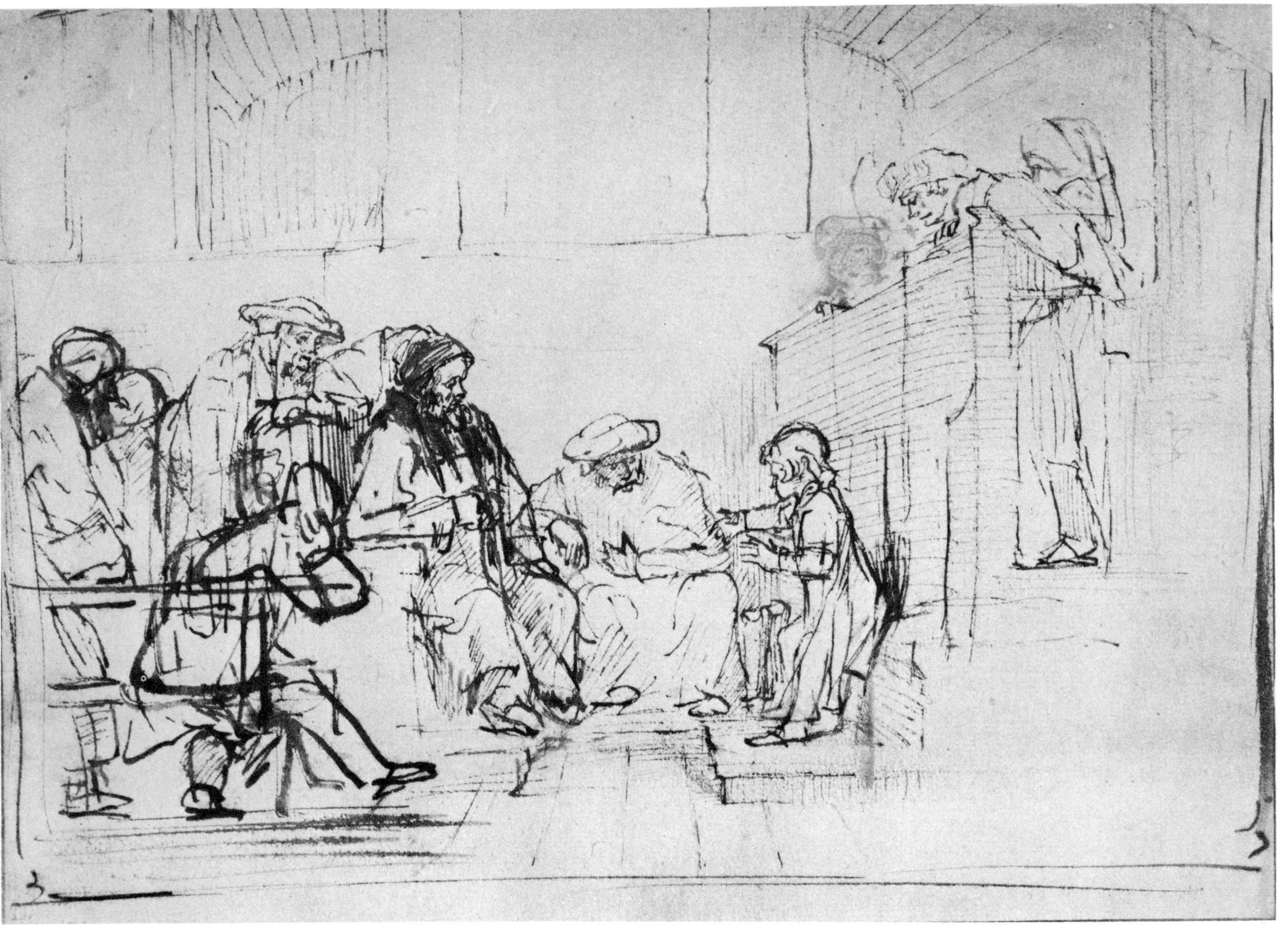

34. Christ in the Temple Disputing with the Doctors. Ca. 1652. Reed pen and bistre, corrections in white body color. 189 x 259 mm. Louvre, Paris.

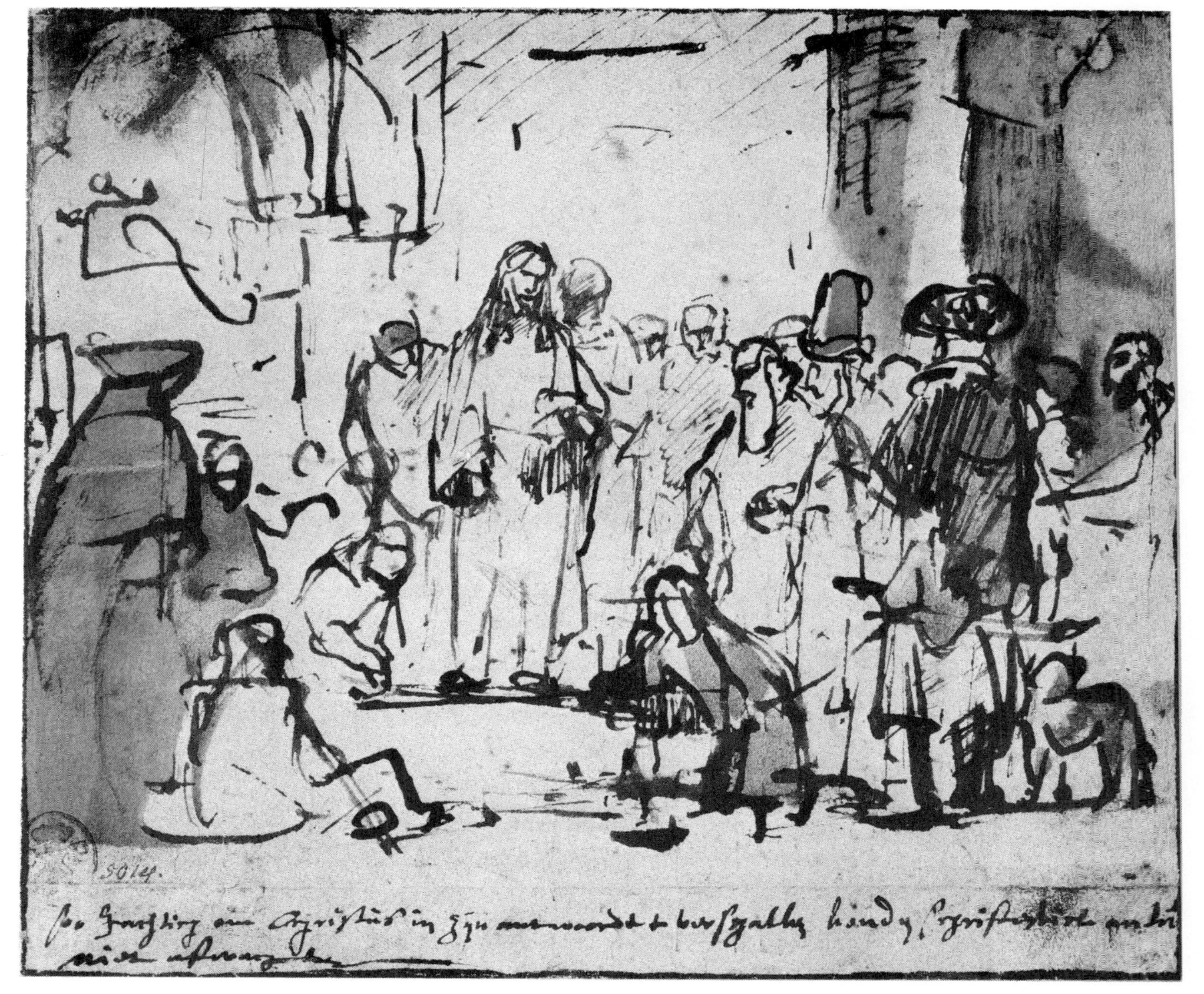

35. Christ and the Woman Taken in Adultery. Ca. 1659. Pen and bistre, red and gray washes added by a later hand. 170 x 202 mm. Staatliche Graphische Sammlung, Munich.

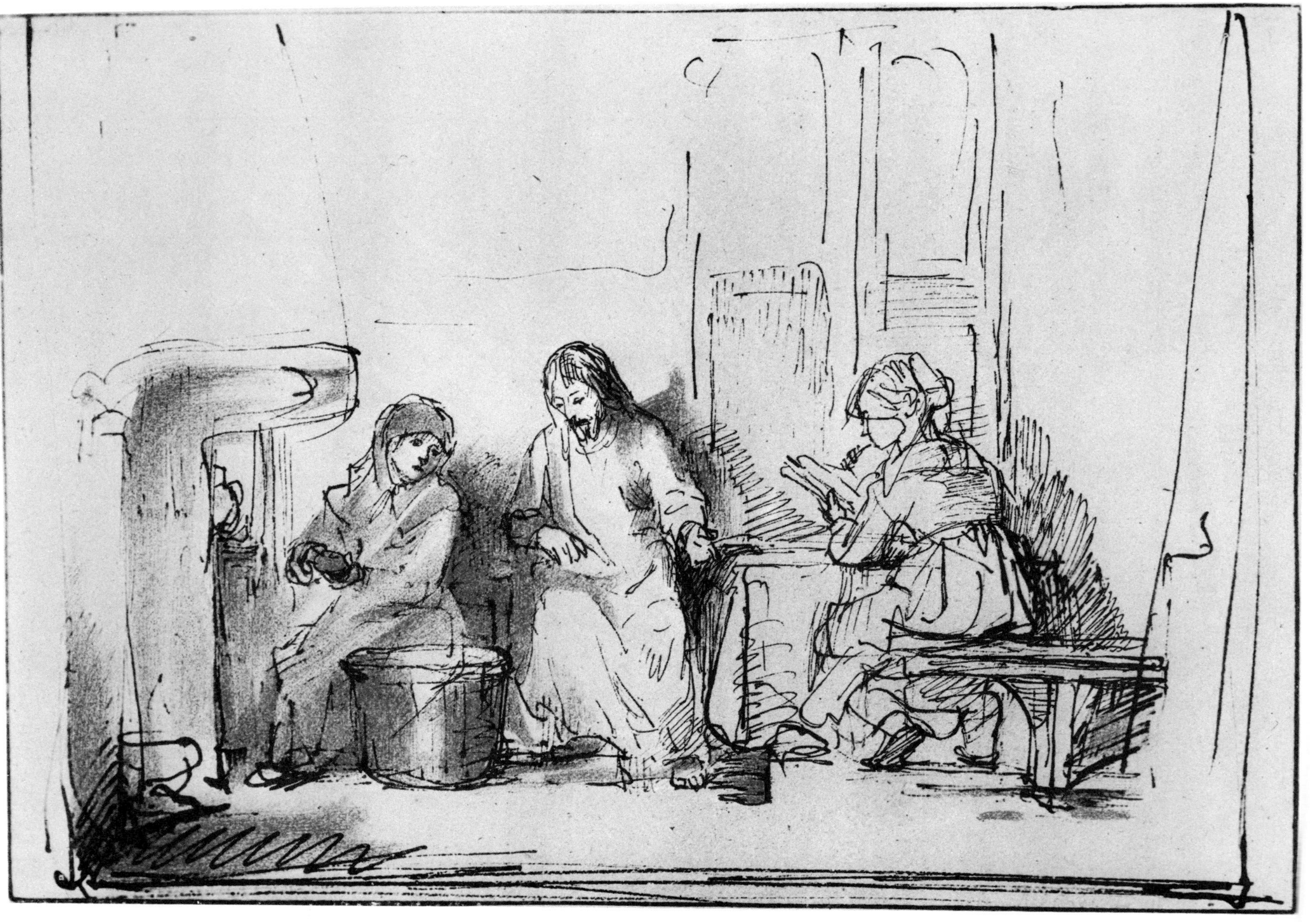

36. Christ Conversing with Mary and Martha. Ca. 1648–50. Pen and wash in bistre. 167 x 233 mm. British Museum, London.

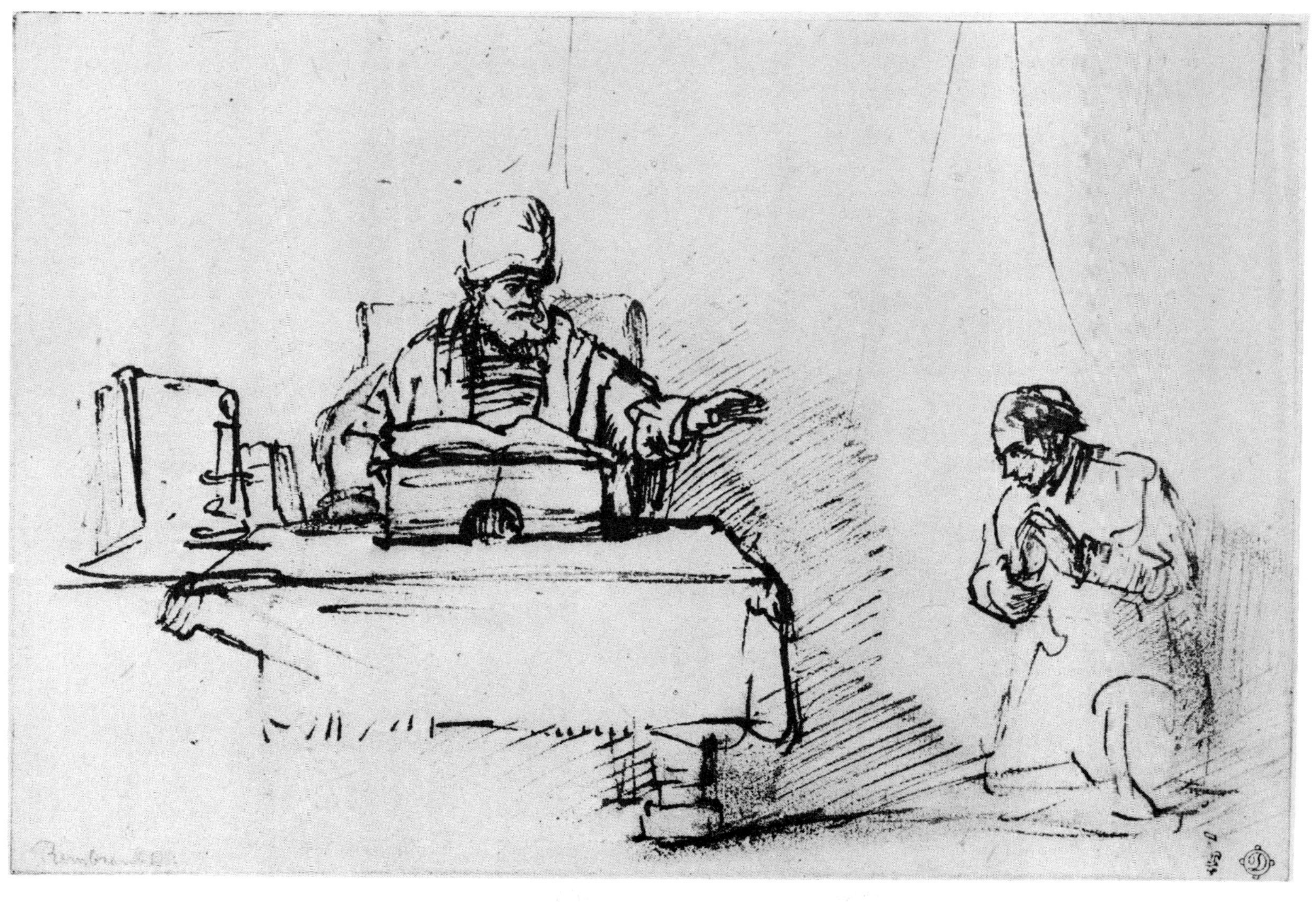

37. The Wicked Servant Begs for Pardon. Ca. 1648–49. Pen and bistre, slightly washed. 140 x 205 mm. Musée Condé, Chantilly.

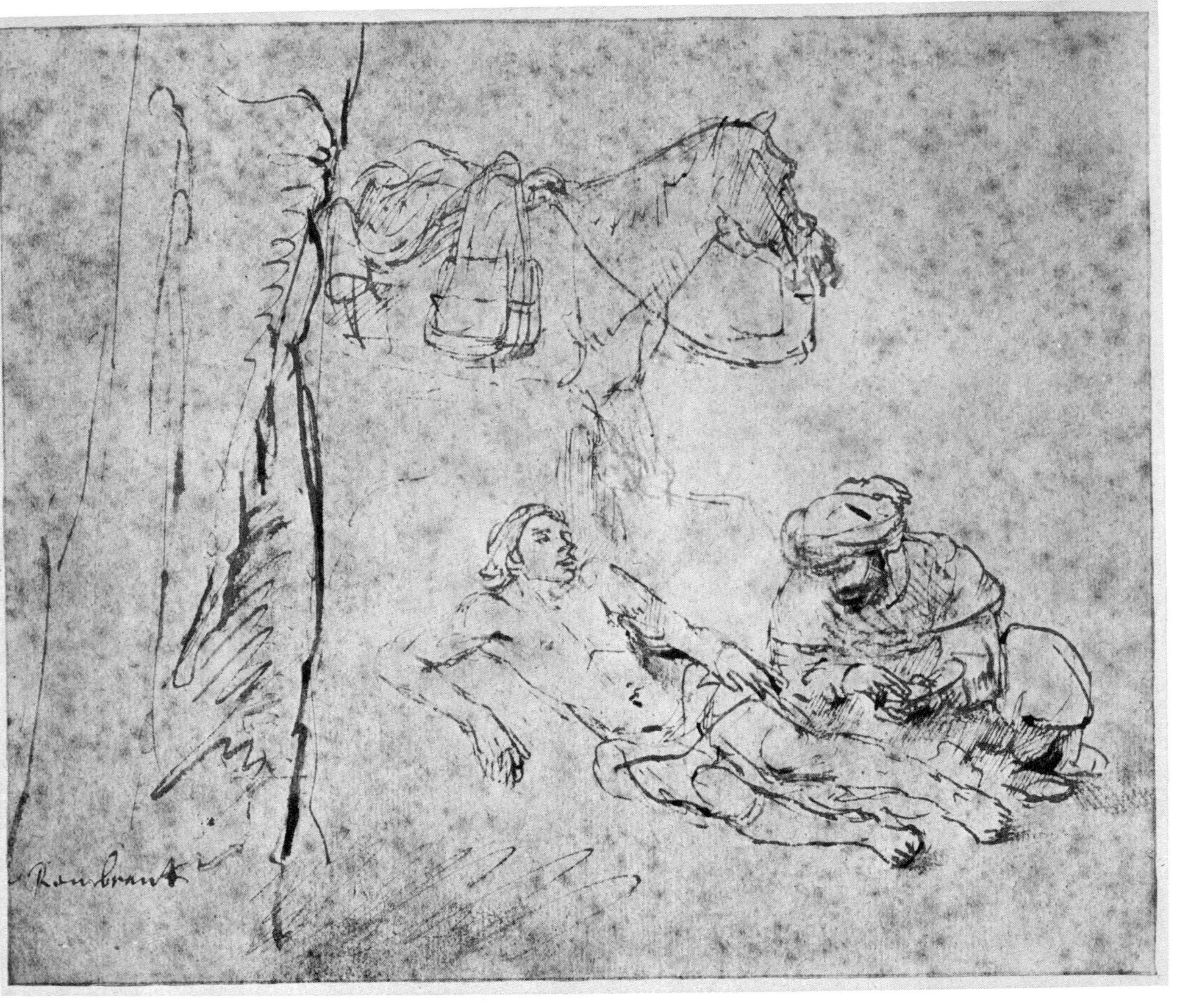

38. The Good Samaritan. Ca. 1650–55. Reed pen and bistre, some white body color. 164 x 195 mm. Kupferstichkabinett, Berlin.

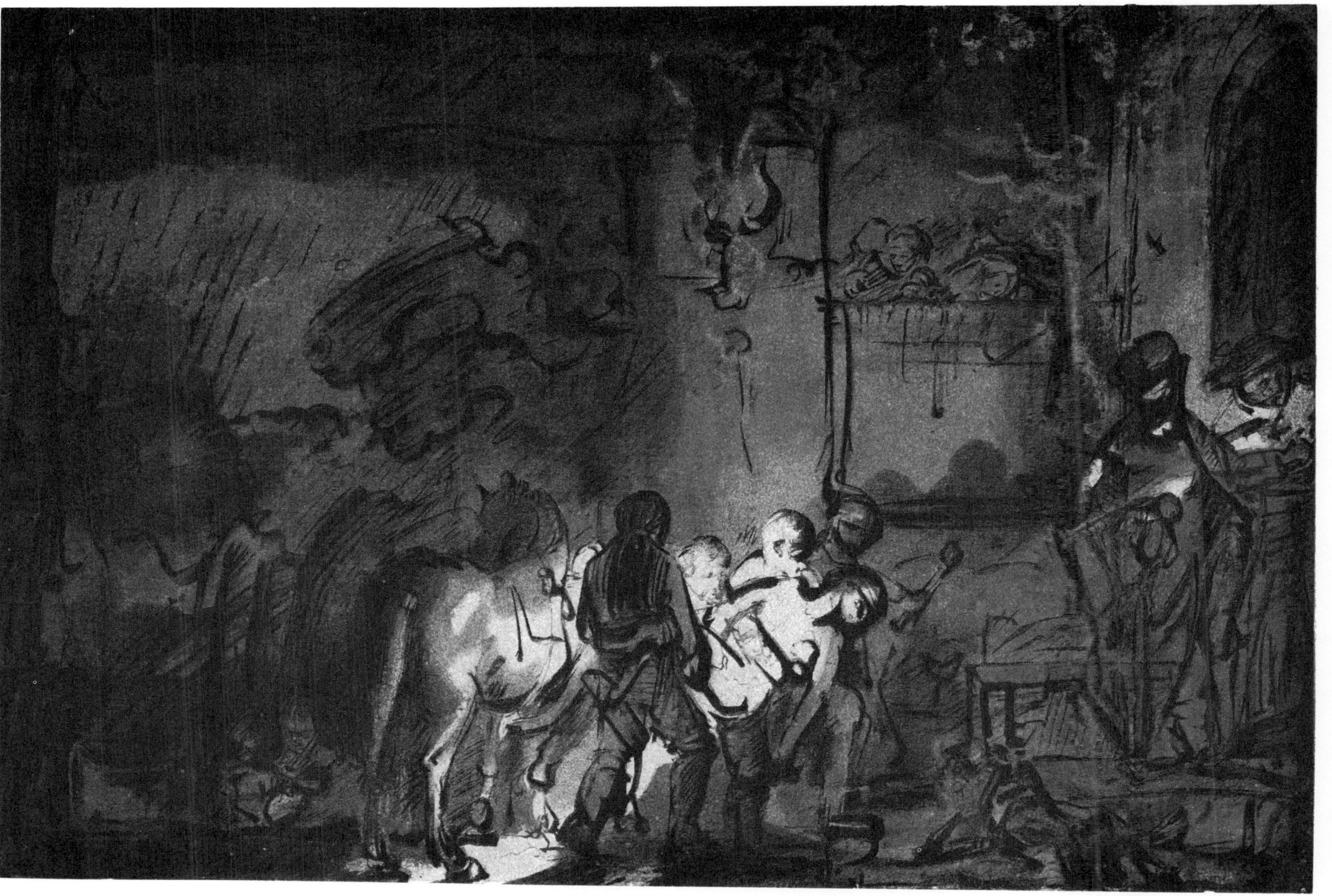

39. The Good Samaritan Bringing the Wounded Man into the Inn. Ca. 1641–43. Pen and wash in bistre, white body color. 209 x 310 mm. Boymans-van Beuningen Museum, Rotterdam.

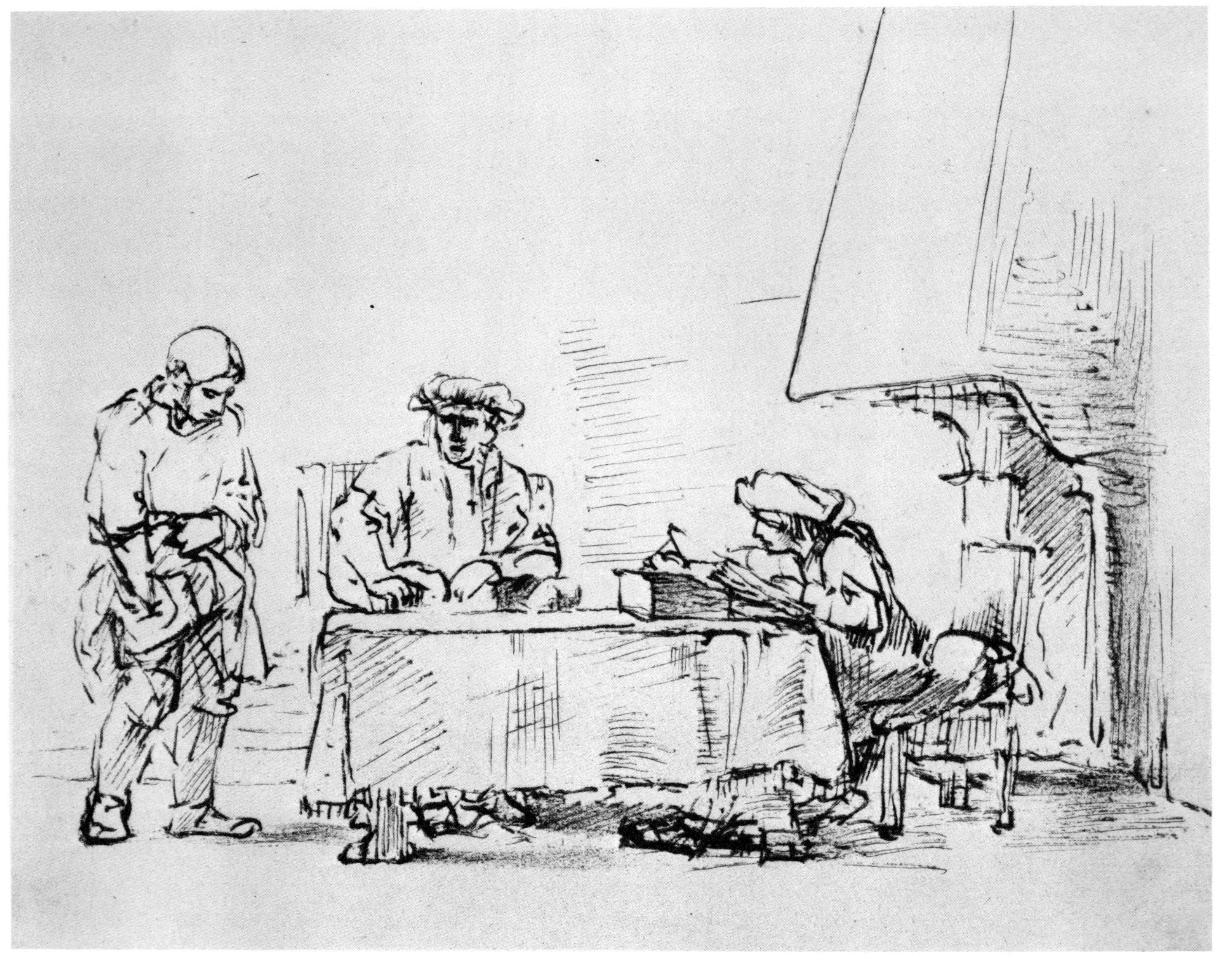

40. The Parable of the Talents. Ca. 1652. Reed pen and bistre. 173 x 218 mm. Louvre, Paris.

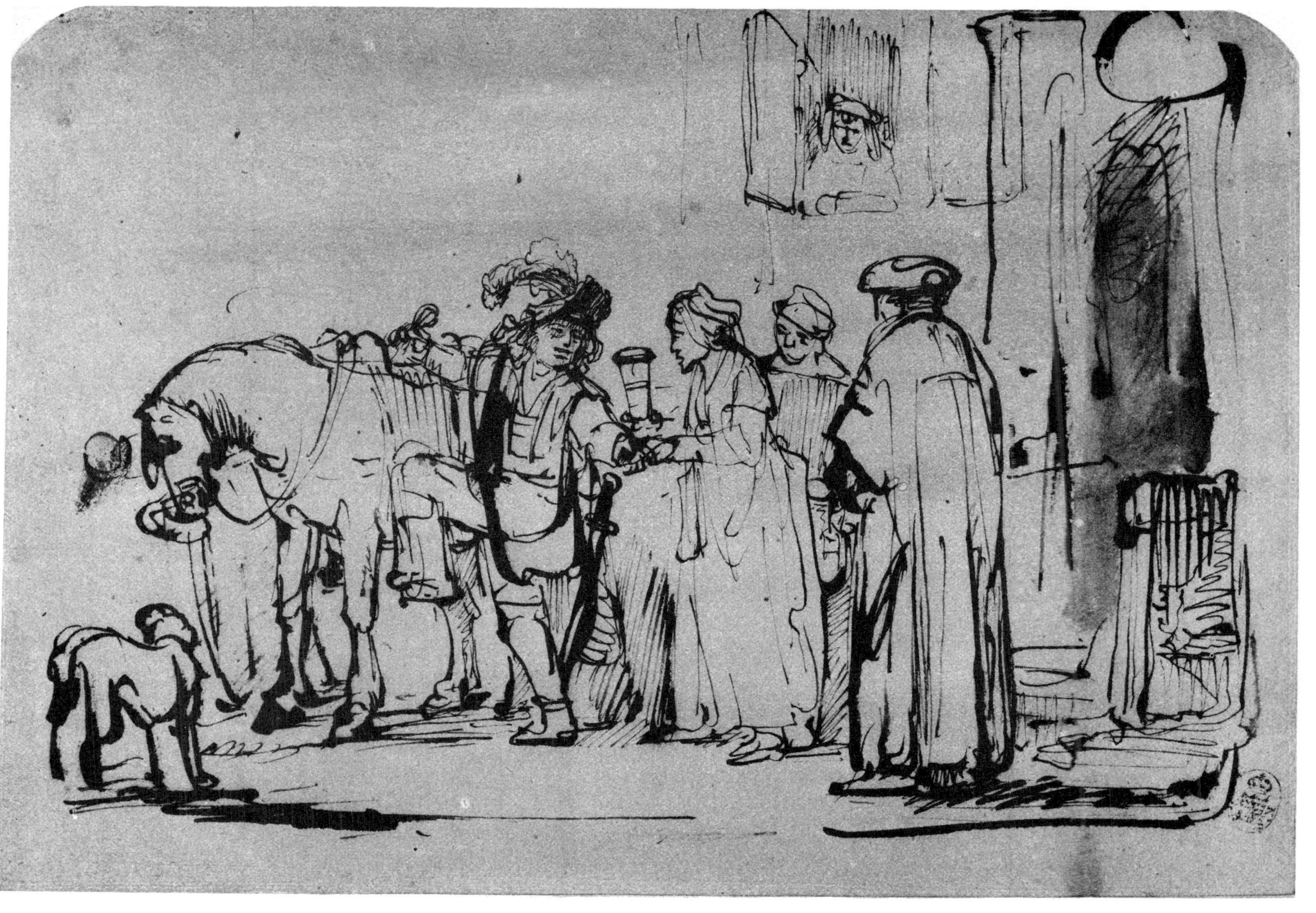

41. The Departure of the Prodigal Son. Ca. 1632–33. Pen, bistre and wash. 193 x 275 mm. Kupferstichkabinett, Dresden.

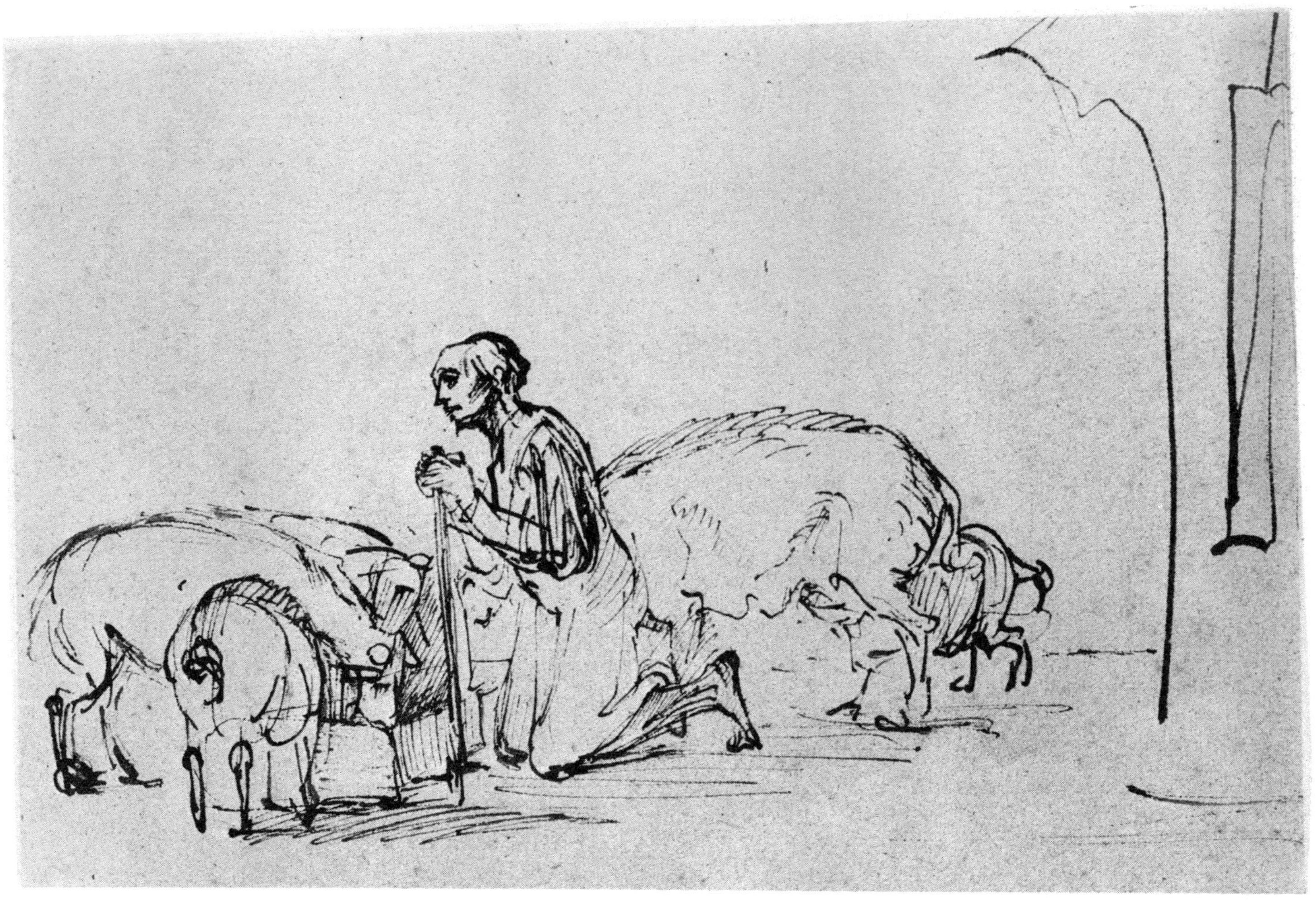

42. THE PRODIGAL SON AMONG THE SWINE. Ca. 1647–48. Pen and bistre. 159 x 235 mm. British Museum, London.

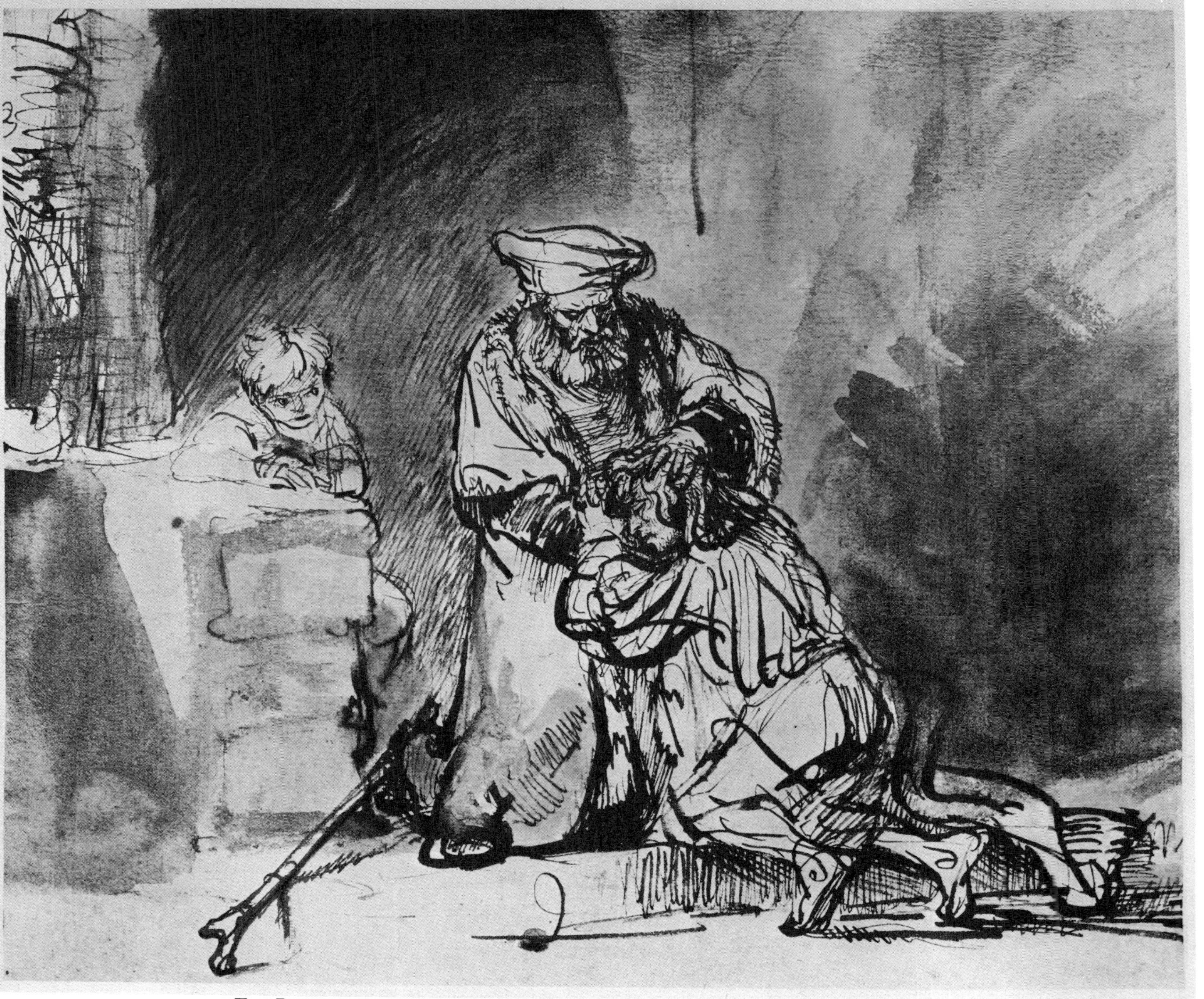

43. The Return of the Prodigal Son. Ca. 1642. Pen and wash in bistre. 190 x 227 mm. Teyler Museum, Haarlem.

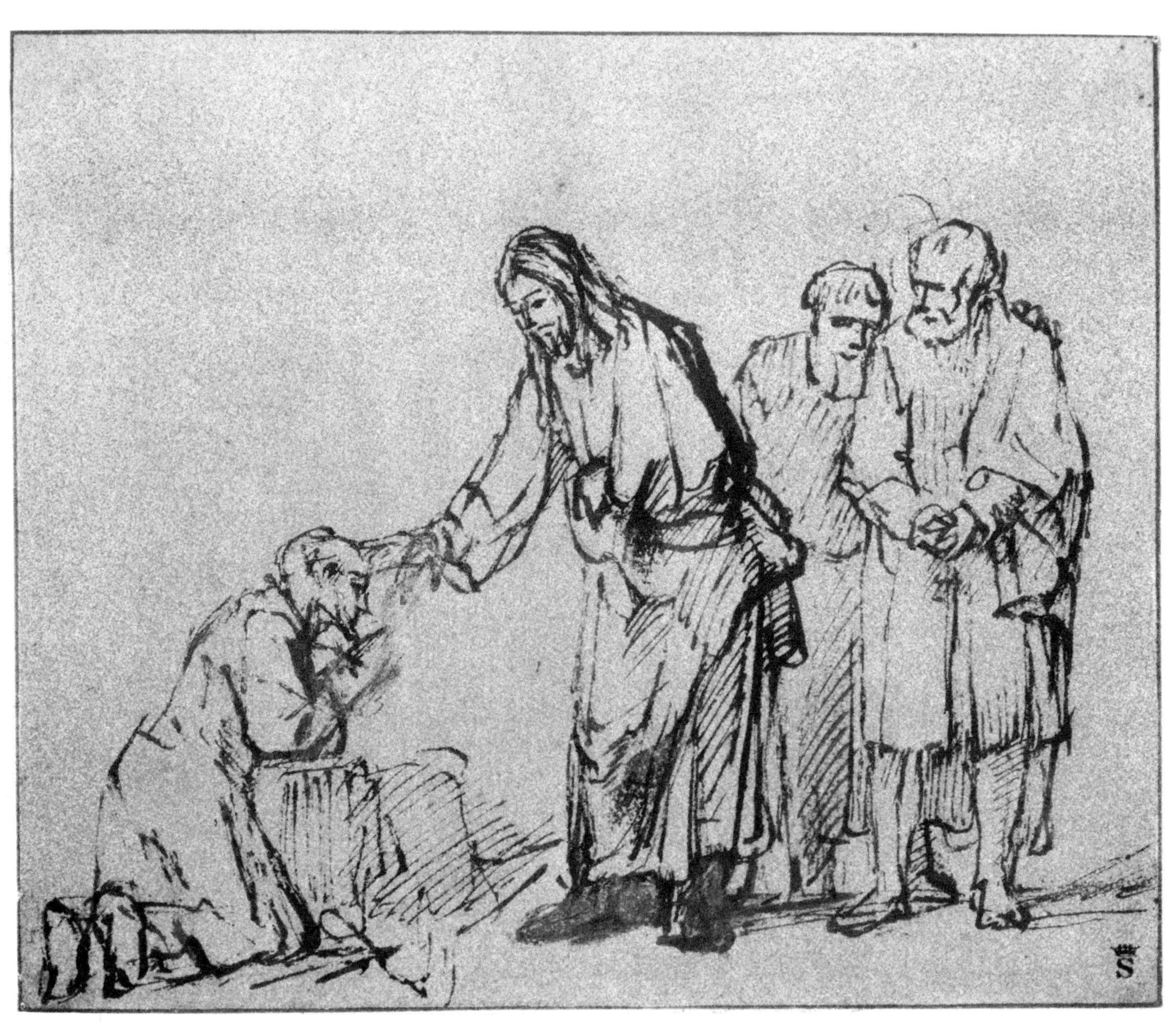

44. CHRIST HEALING A LEPER. Ca. 1657–60. Pen and bistre, white body color. 147 x 172 mm. Rijksprentenkabinet, Amsterdam.

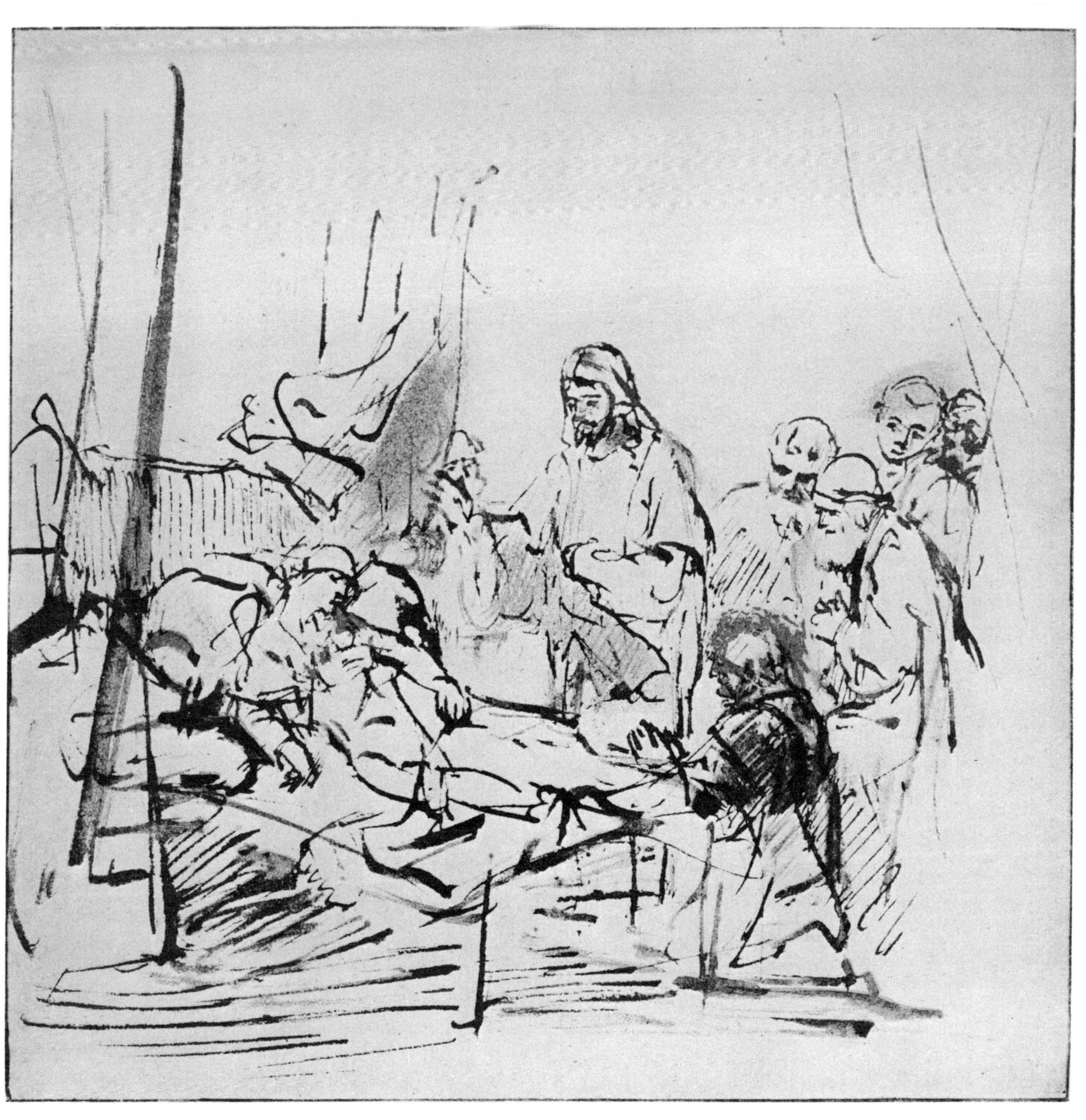

45. The Raising of the Daughter of Jairus. Ca. 1655–60. Pen and bistre, wash, white body color. 198 x 198 mm. Kupferstichkabinett, Berlin.

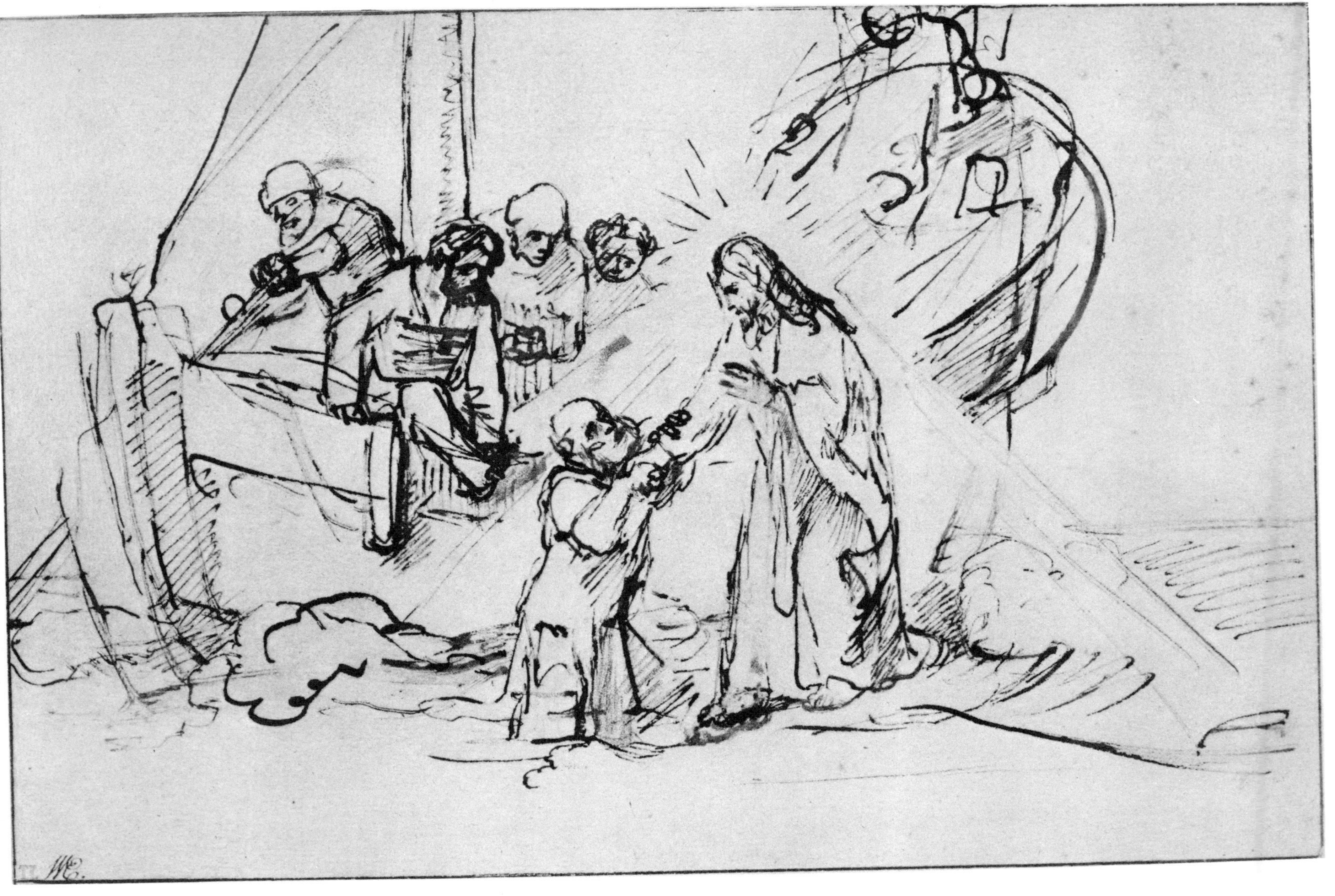

46. Christ Walking on the Waves. Ca. 1658–60. Reed pen and bistre. 191 x 295 mm. British Museum, London.

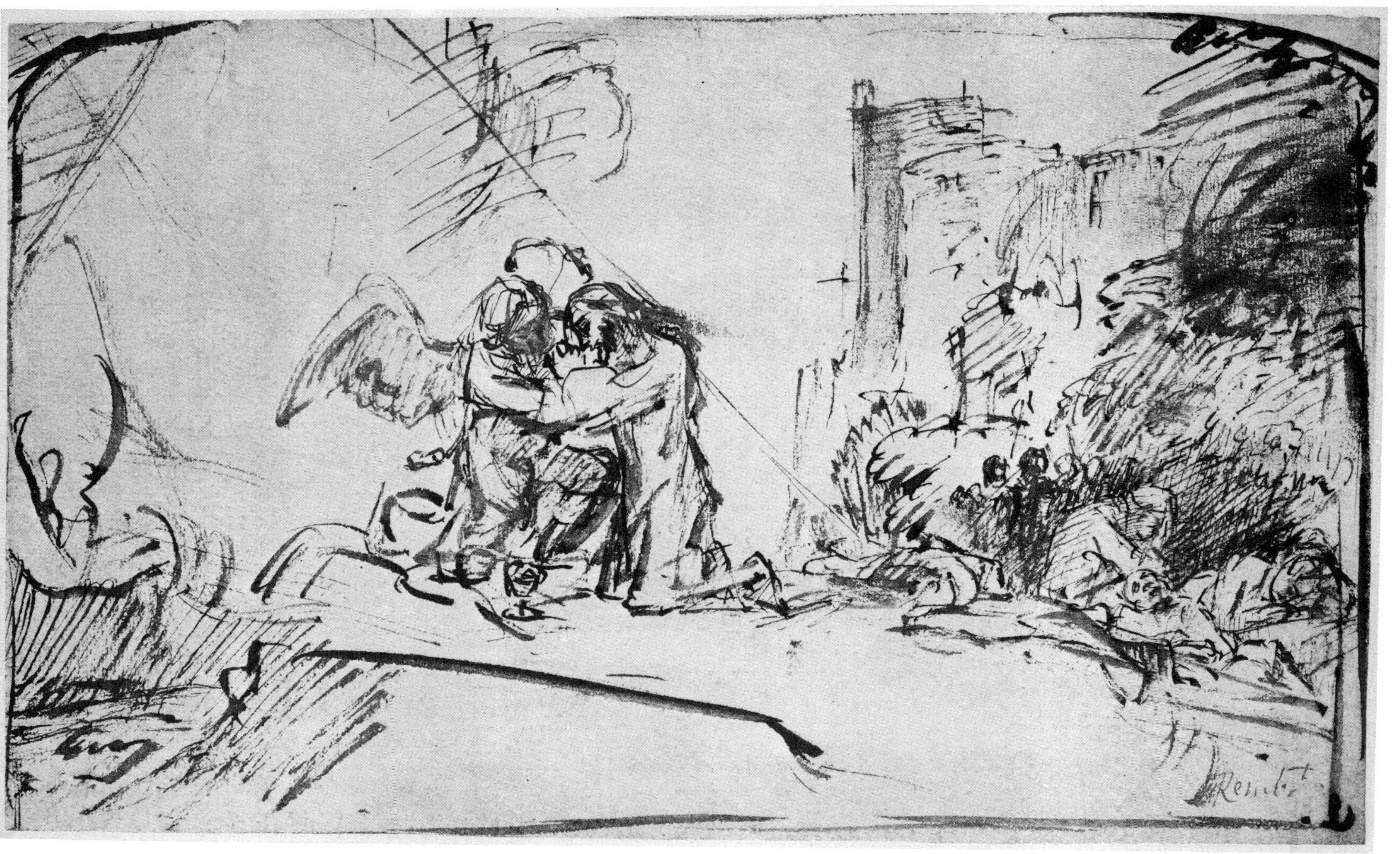

47. Christ Consoled by the Angel on the Mount of Olives. Ca. 1655–57. Pen and bistre, white bcdy color. 184 x 301 mm. Kunsthalle, Hamburg.

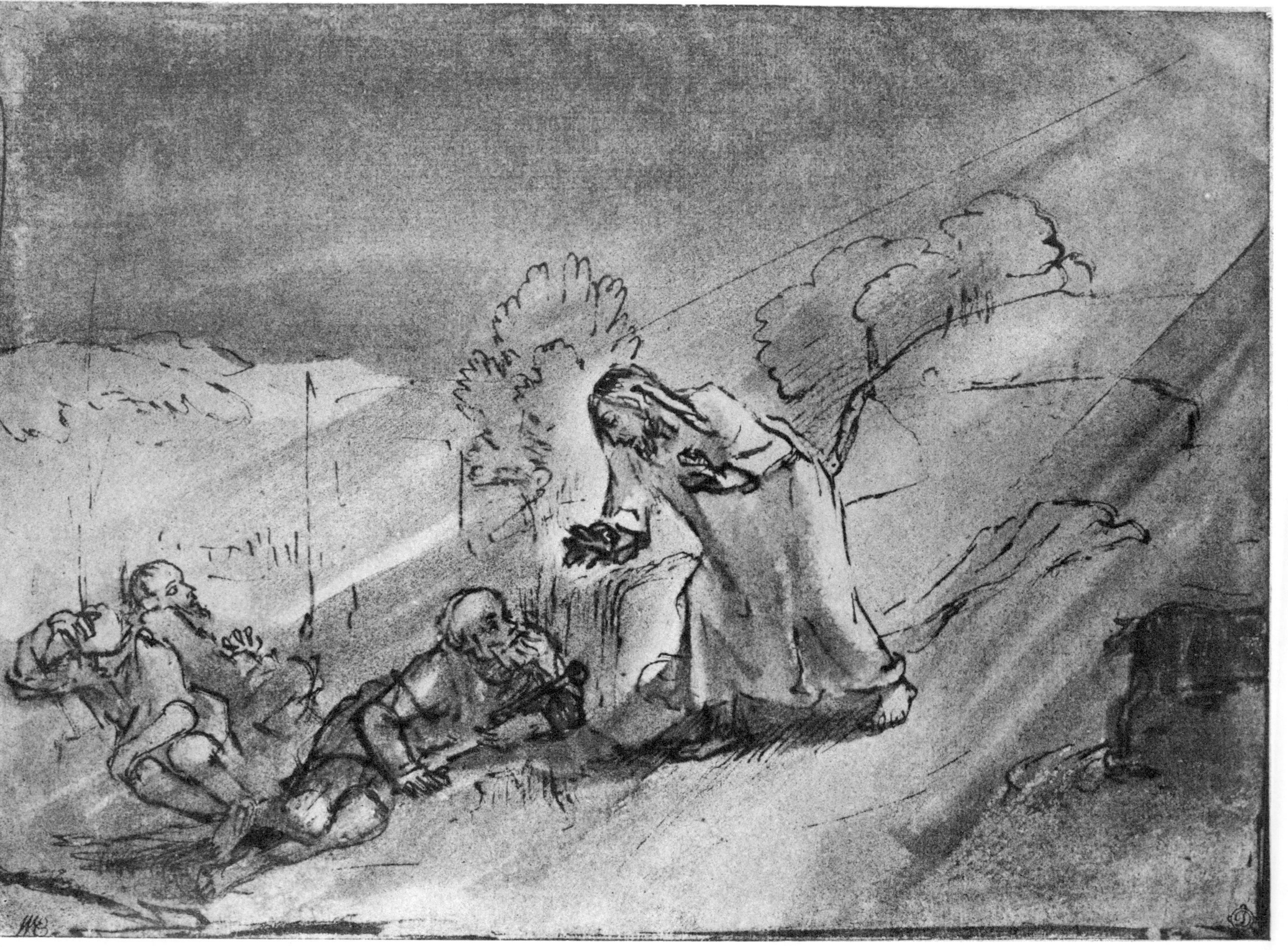

48. Christ Finding His Disciples Asleep on the Mount of Olives. Ca. 1655. Pen and bistre, wash. 178 x 243 mm. Kupferstichkabinett, Berlin.

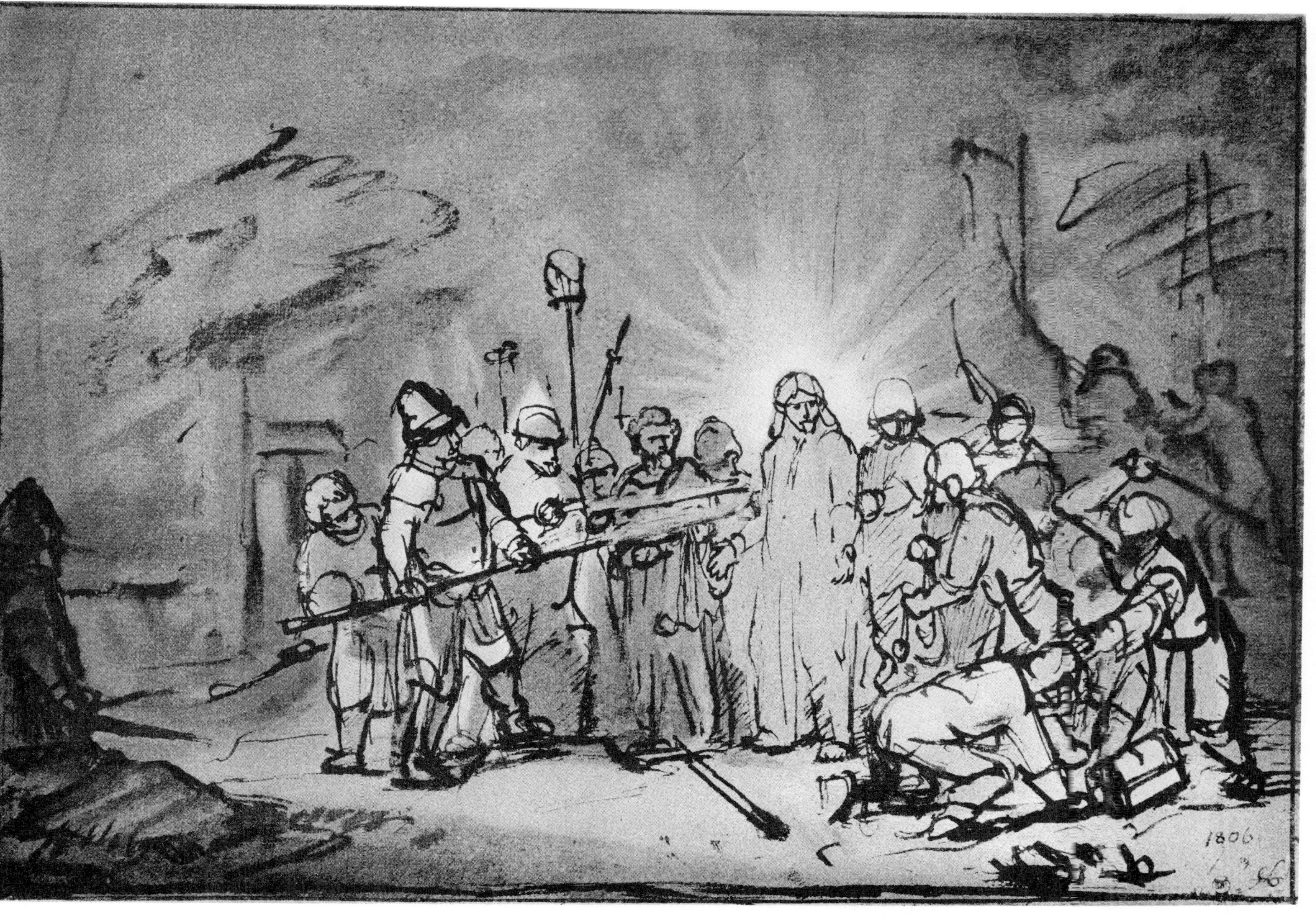

49. The Arrest of Christ. Ca. 1655–60. Pen and wash in bistre. 205 x 298 mm. National-museum, Stockholm.

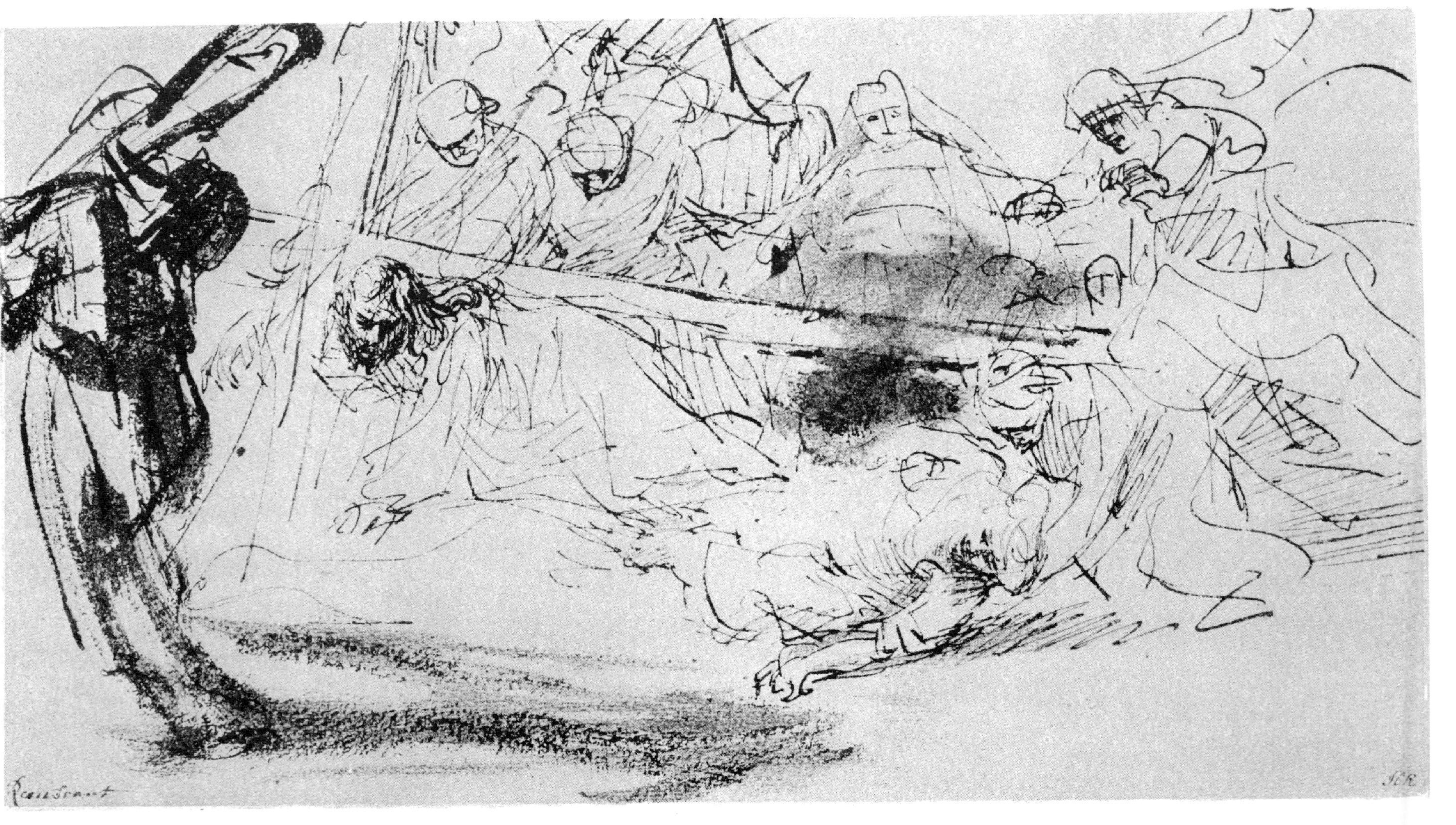

50. Christ Carrying the Cross. Mid-1630s. Pen and bistre, wash. 145 x 260 mm. Kupferstichkabinett, Berlin.

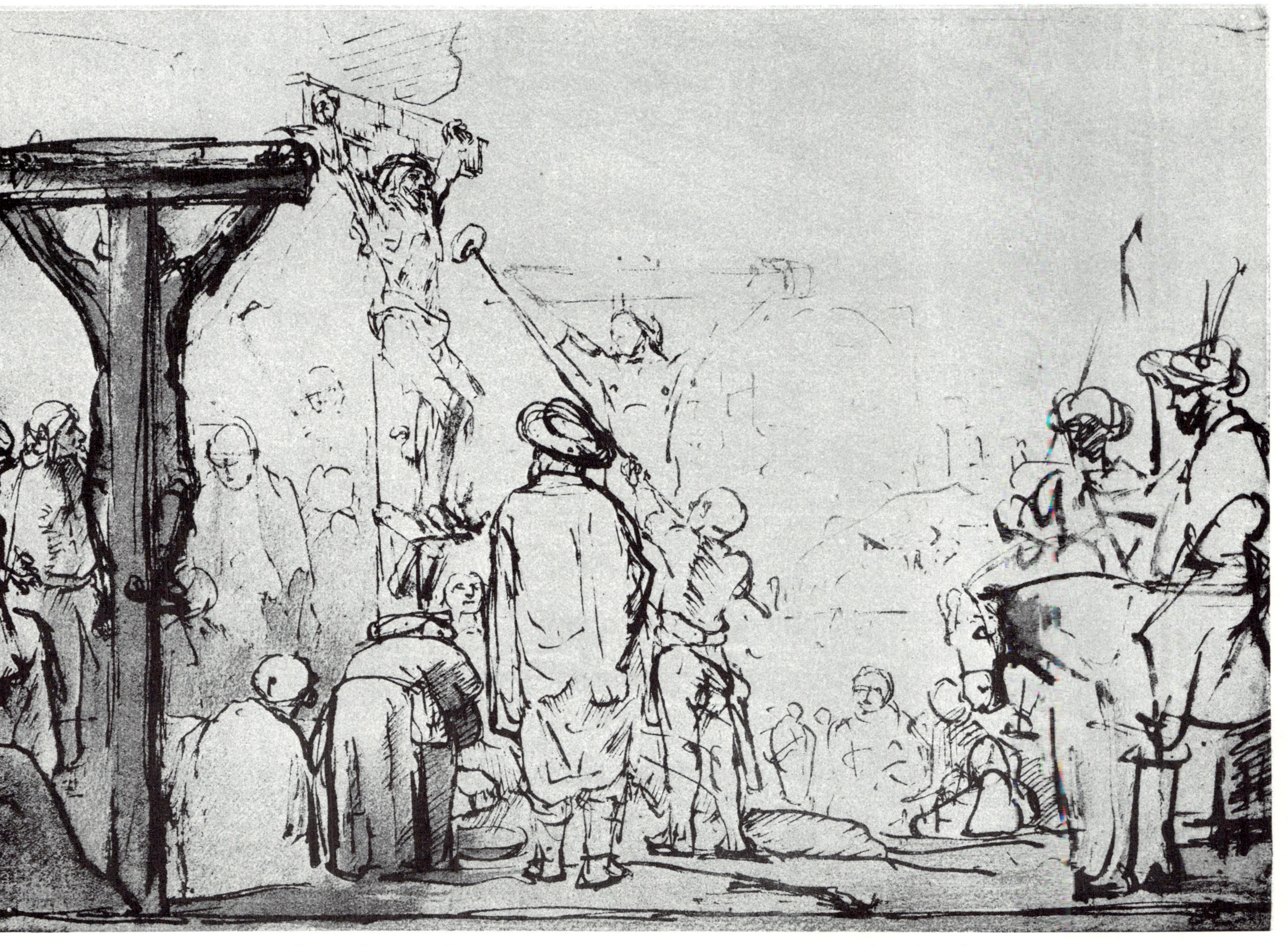

51. Christ Crucified Between the Two Thieves. Ca. 1650–55. Pen and wash in bistre, white body color. 205 x 285 mm. Louvre, Paris.

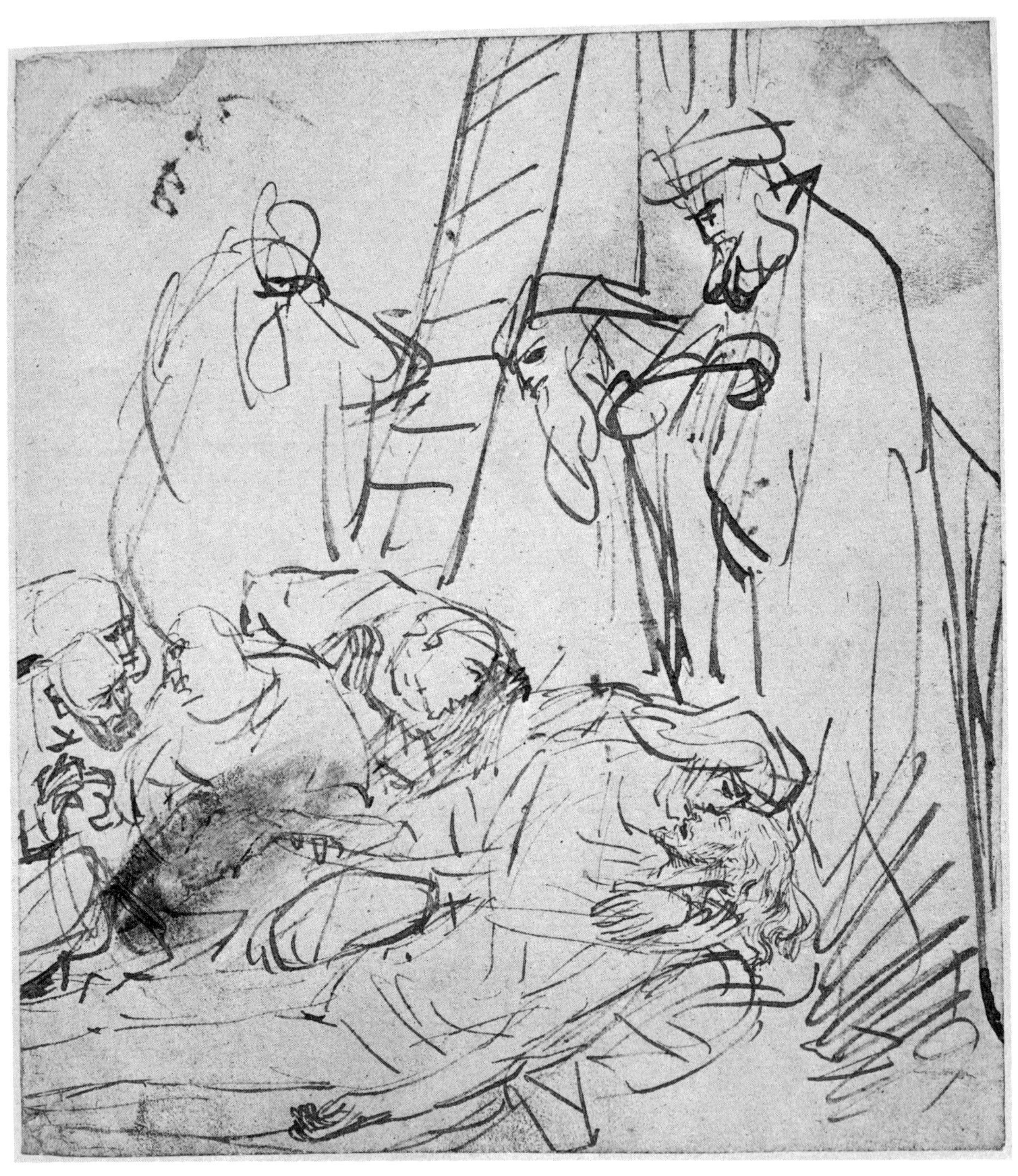

52. The Lamentation Over the Dead Body of Christ. Ca. 1635. Pen and bistre. 171 x 154 mm. Kupferstichkabinett, Berlin.

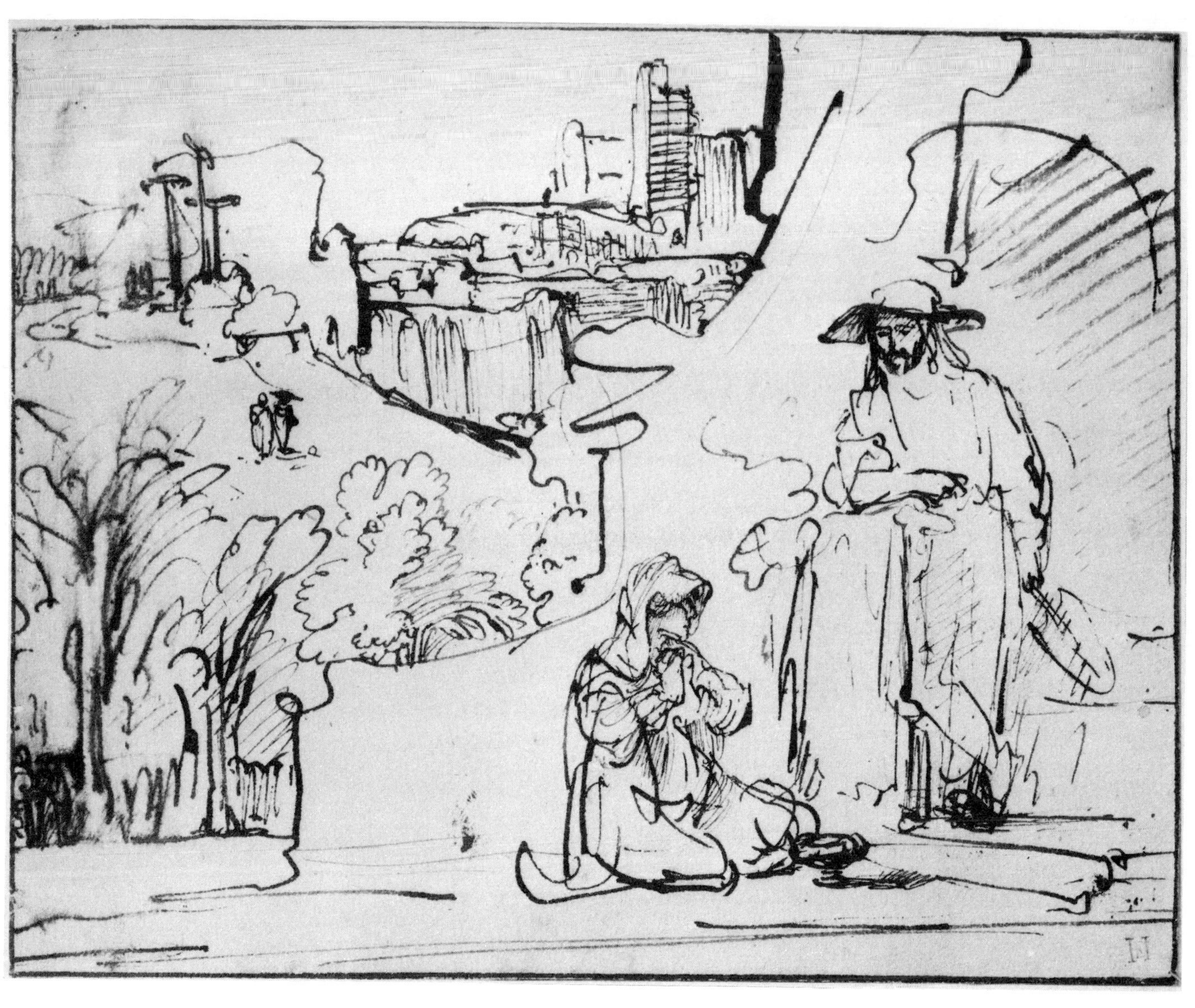

53. Christ Appearing as a Gardener to Mary Magdalen. Ca. 1643. Pen and bistre. 152 x 190 mm. Rijksprentenkabinet, Amsterdam.

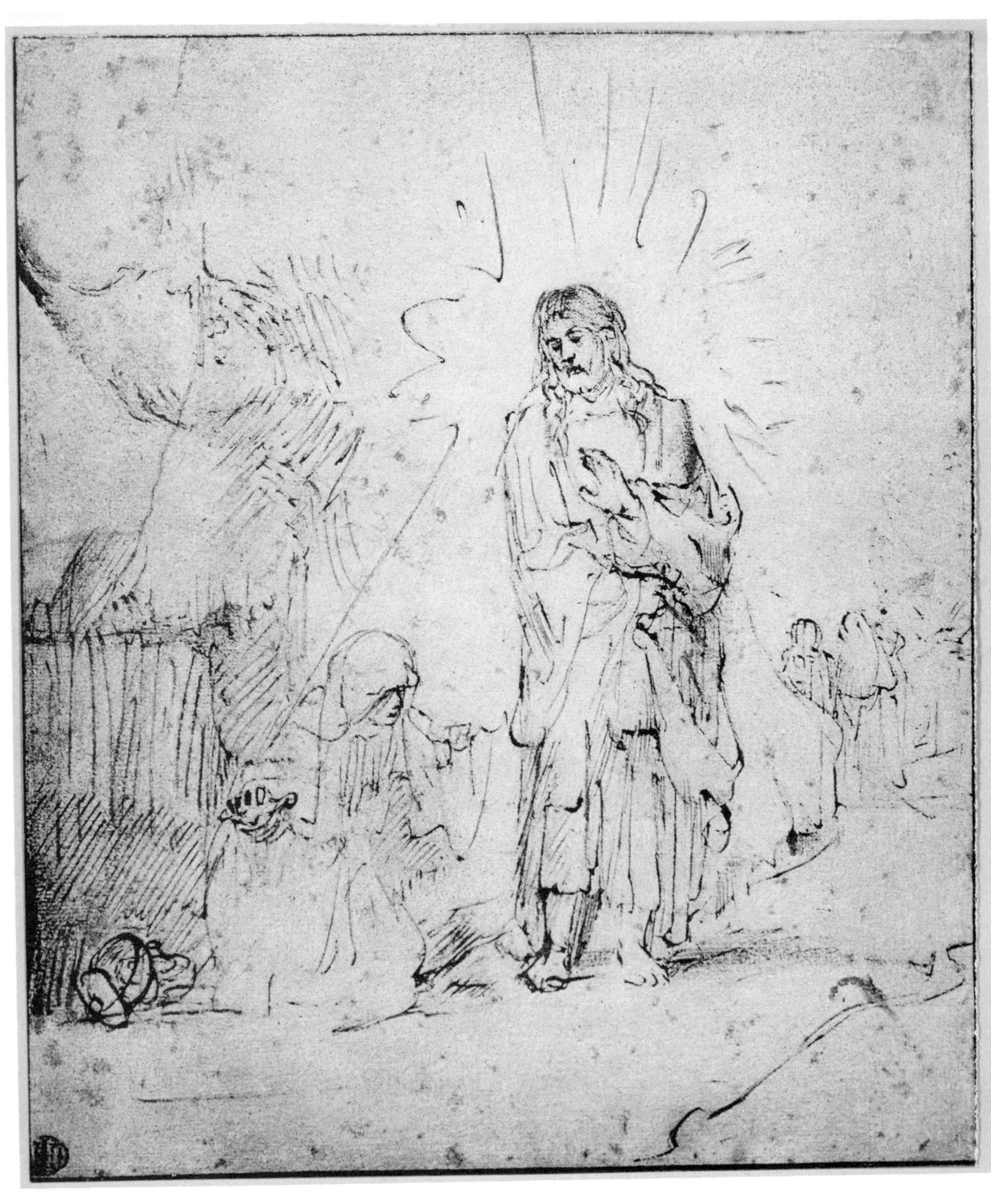

54. Noli Me Tangere. Ca. 1650. Pen and bistre. 220 x 185 mm. Van de Waals Collection, Heemstede.

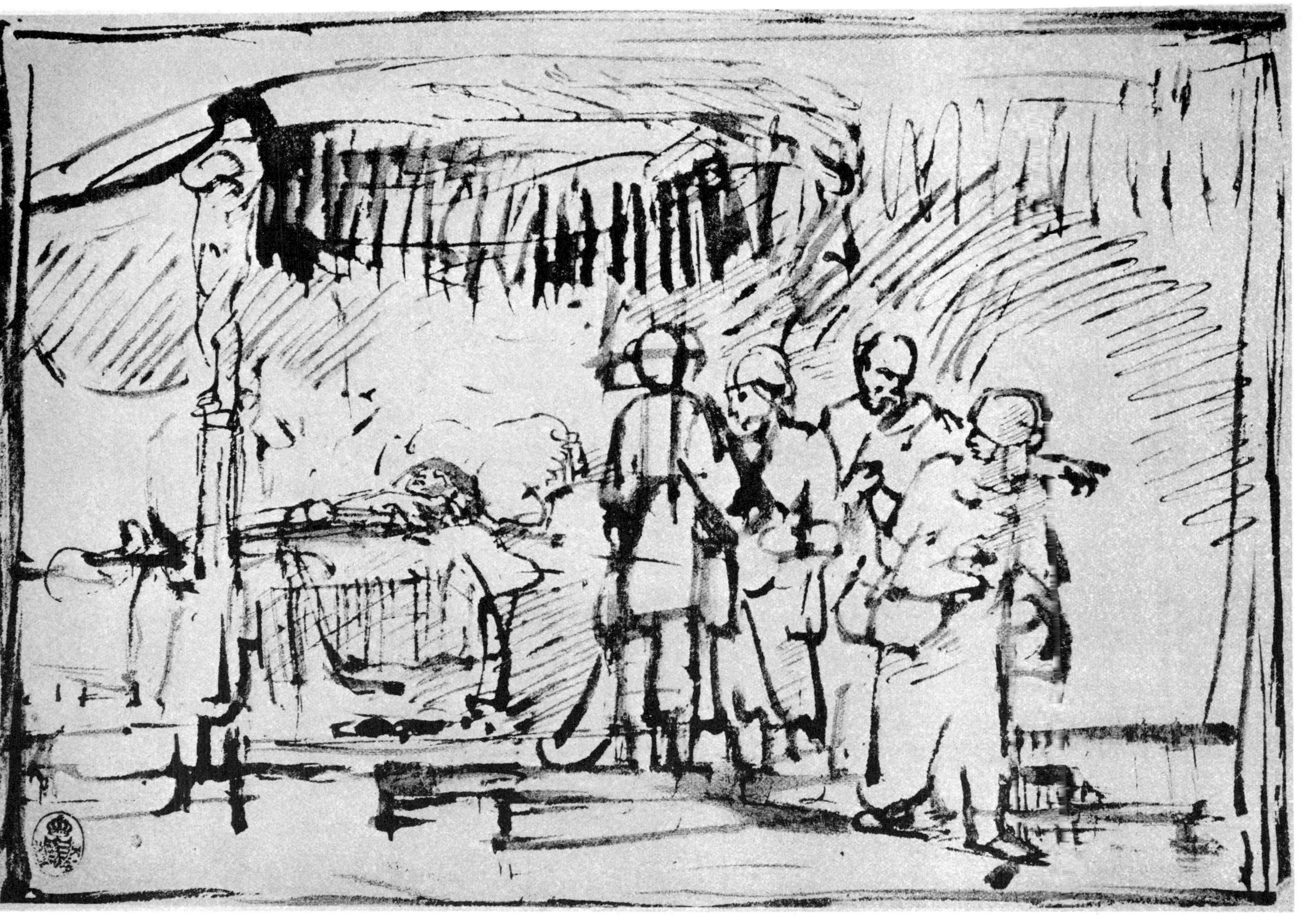

55. St. Peter at the Deathbed of Tabitha. Ca. 1660–65. Reed pen and bistre. 190 × 273 mm. Kupferstichkabinett, Dresden.

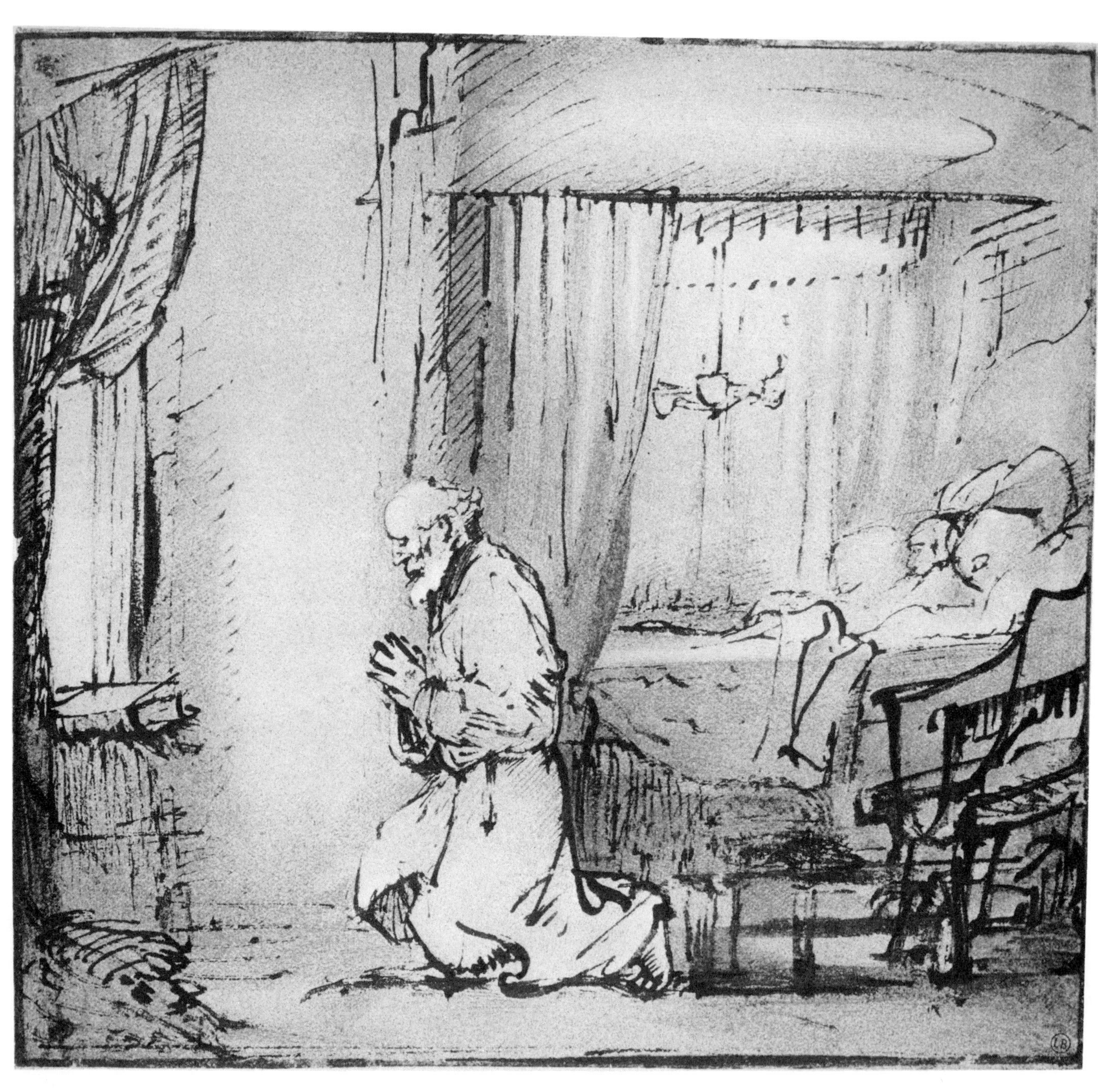

56. St. Peter's Prayer Before the Raising of Tabitha. Ca. 1655–60. Reed pen and wash, white body color. 190 x 200 mm. Musée, Bayonne.

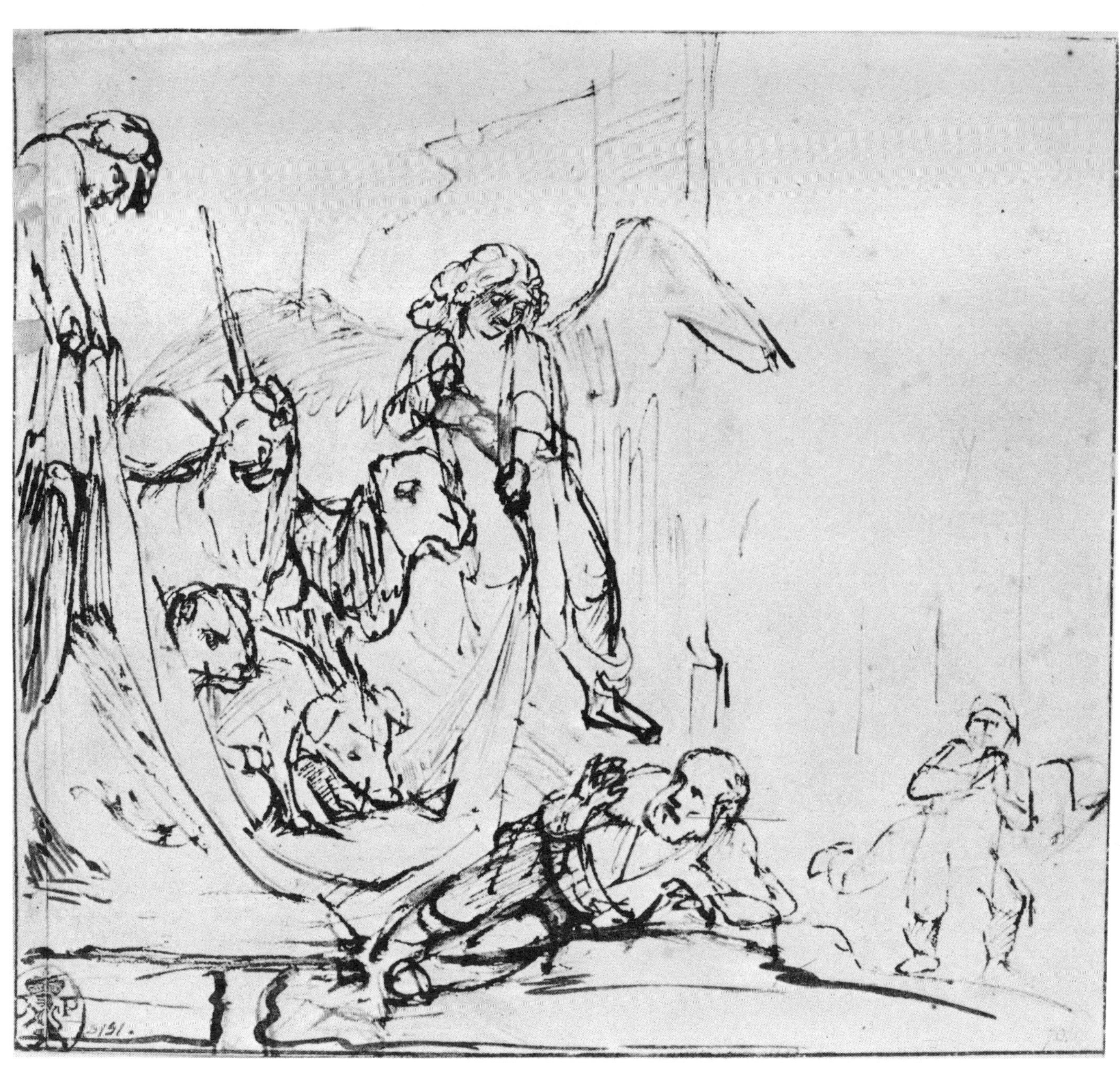

57. THE VISION OF ST. PETER. Ca. 1660. Pen and bistre. 179 x 193 mm. Staatliche Graphische Sammlung, Munich.

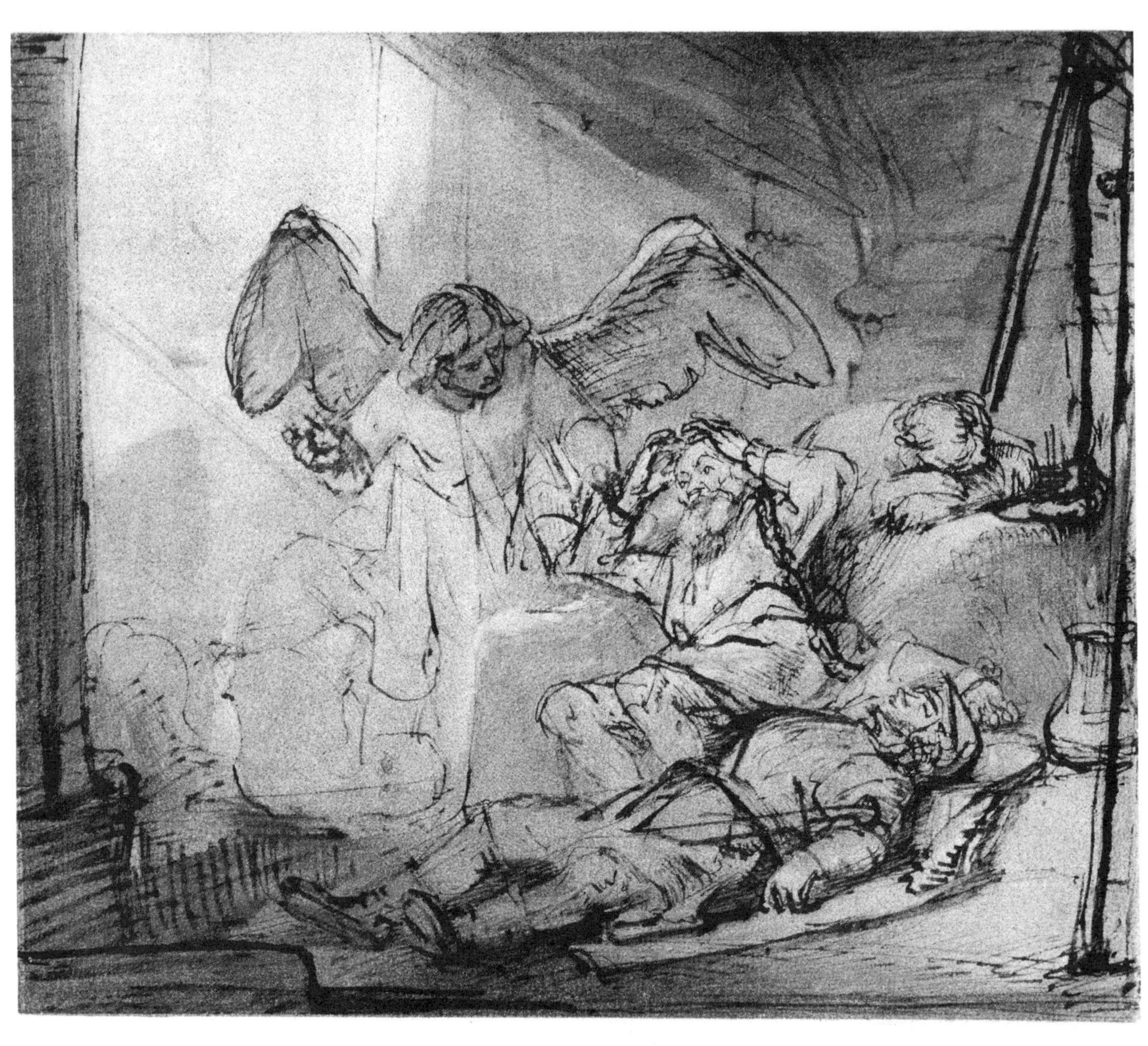

58. The Liberation of St. Peter from Prison. Ca. 1648–49. Pen and wash in bistre. 195 x 221 mm. Städelsches Kunstinstitut, Frankfurt a/M.

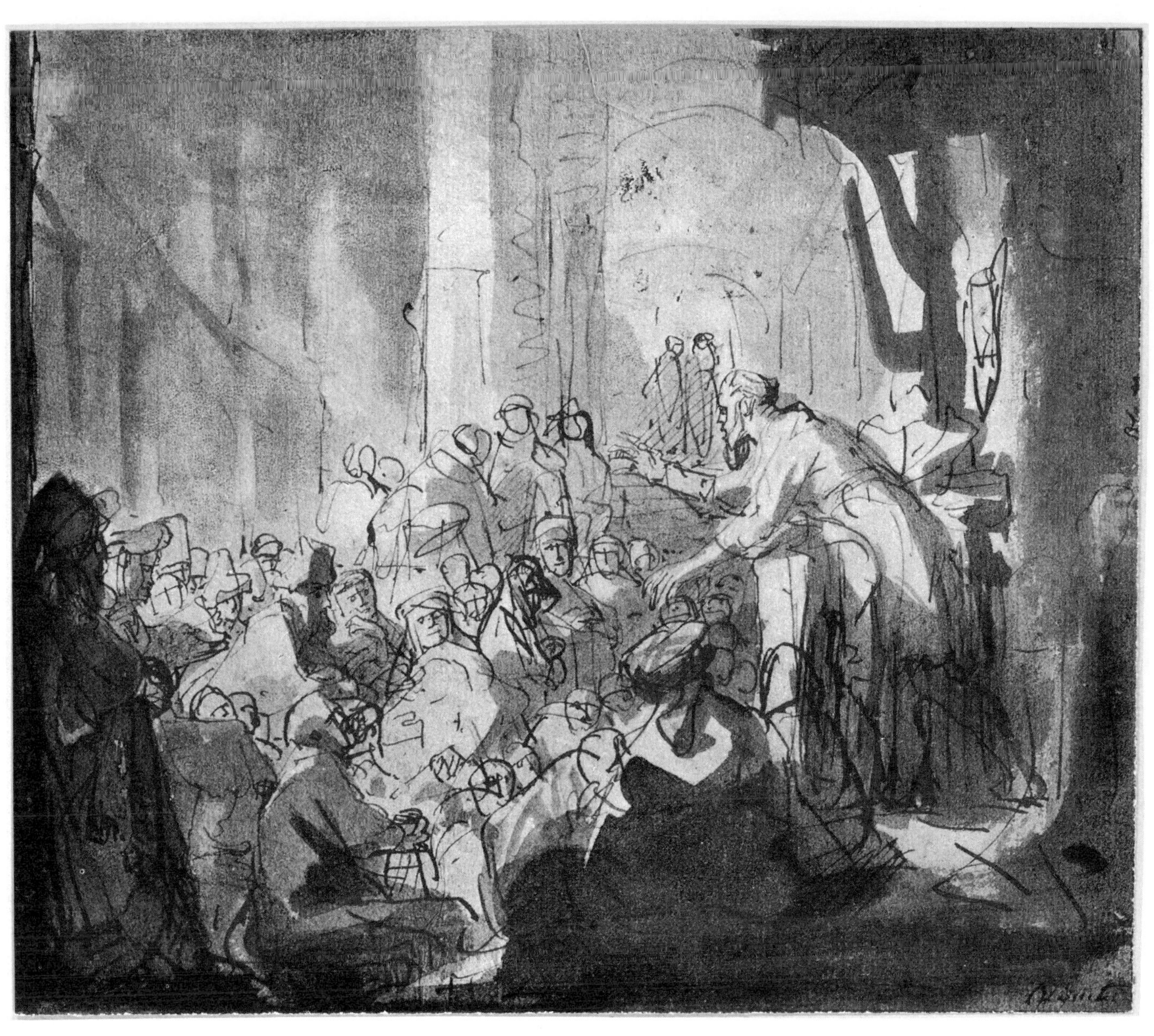

59. St. Paul Preaching at Athens. Ca. 1637. Pen and bistre, wash. 178 x 204 mm. British Museum, London.